Copyright © 2024 by Edenbrook Learning, LLC

All rights reserved, including the right to reproduce, distribute, or transmit this work in any form or by any means, electronic or mechanical, including photocopying, recording, or by any information storage and retrieval system, without express written permission from the copyright holder, except as permitted under "fair use" clauses of copyright law.

International Standard Book Number (ISBN): 9798344208091
Second Edition: 2024
Publisher: Edenbrook Learning, LLC

Disclaimer: This book is designed to provide information and education. SAT is a trademark registered by the College board, which is not affiliated with, and does not endorse, this product.

Permissions: You may quote small portions of this book for educational purposes, provided that you credit the author and publisher. You may not reproduce any substantial portion of the book without written permission from the copyright holder.

TABLE OF CONTENTS

TEST 1

Module 1 1
Module 2 11
Scoring Key 22
Answer Explanations 23

TEST 2

Module 1 33
Module 2 43
Scoring Key 55
Answer Explanations 56

TEST 3

Module 1 70
Module 2 80
Scoring Key 92
Answer Explanations 93

TEST 4

Module 1 107
Module 2 119
Scoring Key 130
Answer Explanations 131

Reading and Writing
32 MINUTES, 27 QUESTIONS

DIRECTIONS

The questions in this section address a number of important reading and writing skills. Each question includes one or more passages, which may include a table or graph. Read each passage and question carefully, and then choose the best answer to the question based on the passage(s).

All questions in this section are multiple-choice with four answer choices. Each question has a single best answer.

1

Although space shuttles must carry only the bare necessities for an effective lift-off, some important components and devices require _____ sets; in the case of malfunction or destruction, this redundancy will enable the system to continue functioning.

Which choice completes the text with the most logical and precise word or phrase?

A) expensive
B) regressive
C) identical
D) dynamic

2

Planned obsolescence refers to a business strategy in which a product is deliberately designed to have a limited useful life; this can be done by using materials prone to _____ after a calculated number of uses so that customers would have to purchase a new device.

Which choice completes the text with the most logical and precise word or phrase?

A) degradation
B) durability
C) resistance
D) amiability

Edenbrook Test 1

3

The life of Harry Potter resembles that of the author, J.K. Rowling. Although Rowling is fabulously _____ as one of the wealthiest women today, for years, she suffered under the scourges of poverty and adversity.

Which choice completes the text with the most logical and precise word or phrase?

A) affluent
B) transcendent
C) fabricated
D) prodigal

4

Dr. Sarah Thompson, a renowned geologist, found herself captivated by an enigmatic outcropping. The geologist scrutinized the rock formation, trying to <u>decide</u> its origin. The layers of sediment and the presence of unique minerals made it a challenging task, but she was resolute in unraveling the mystery of the landscape before her.

As used in the text, what does the word "decide" most nearly mean?

A) accept
B) choose
C) select
D) determine

5

While the invention of the printing press greatly expanded access to knowledge, it also had the unintended consequence of _____ the craft of calligraphy, as the handwritten word was no longer the primary means of textual reproduction.

Which choice completes the text with the most logical and precise word or phrase?

A) elevating
B) denigrating
C) supplanting
D) reverberating

6

The following text is from Langston Hughs' 1922 poem "Mother to Son."

Life for me ain't been no crystal stair.
It's had tacks in it,
And splinters,
And boards torn up,
And places with no carpet on the floor—
Bare.
But all the time
I'se been a-climbin' on,
And reachin' landin's,
And turnin' corners,
And sometimes goin' in the dark
Where there ain't been no light.

Which choice best states the main purpose of the text?

A) To emphasize the struggles the mother has faced in life
B) To encourage her son to give up in the face of adversity
C) To complain about the unfairness of her difficult life
D) To convey her experiences and persistent determination

7

In Ireland, seanchaí have long served as keepers of folklore, myths, and legends within their communities. They have passed down oral traditions from generation to generation by telling stories of heroes, Celtic gods, and fantastical creatures. Although books and digital media allow information to be recorded in new ways, seanchaí continue to practice their storytelling craft. Their lively retellings still entertain and remind people of their cultural heritage.

Which choice best states the main idea of the text?

A) Seanchaí tell stories of heroes, Celtic gods, and fantastical creatures, which are the main components of the folklore they preserve.

B) Books and digital media have replaced the need for seanchaí, making their storytelling craft irrelevant in modern times.

C) Oral traditions play a crucial role in helping communities maintain their cultural identity, regardless of the presence of seanchaí.

D) Seanchaí continue to practice their storytelling, keeping its cultural heritage alive despite the availability of new forms of record keeping.

8

The following text is from a novel about life in the Midwest. The following describes the setting of an annual event.

It was that time of year again on the Bar Ranch. Every spring, the ranchers inspected their cattle herd to check for health issues before driving the cows up to the mountain pastures. Now the ranchers began to inspect the cattle—walking calmly among them, lasso in hand, choosing an animal to rope and examine. The cows, like people, have their individual temperaments; some were docile and cooperative while others were more stubborn. One by one, a cow was led into the holding pen and thoroughly looked over for injuries or illness. The ranchers took their time, carefully evaluating each animal before releasing it to rejoin the herd.

Which choice best describes the function of the underlined sentence in the text as a whole?

A) It describes the ranchers conducting their health inspection before moving to the mountains.

B) It elaborates on some aspects of the cows that the ranchers assess.

C) It illustrates the diverse skills and techniques used by the ranchers as they work.

D) It emphasizes the strong similarities between ranchers and their cattle.

9

In 2023, University of Cambridge researchers unveiled "quantum memristors," nanoscale devices that bridge quantum computing and neuromorphic engineering. These devices mimic biological neurons by operating on a continuous spectrum of states, leveraging quantum superposition. Like synapses, quantum memristors can simultaneously store and process information, exhibiting non-linear resistance characteristics. This neuron-like behavior, combined with quantum properties, allows for more complex information processing than traditional binary systems. In quantum neural network simulations, these devices demonstrated a remarkable ability to handle entangled quantum states, potentially enabling more efficient quantum algorithms.

According to the text, how do memristors resemble biological neurons?

A) They demonstrate an ability to handle entangled quantum states in simulations.

B) They exhibit non-linear resistance characteristics during information processing.

C) They operate on a continuous spectrum of states through the use of quantum superposition.

D) They potentially enable more efficient quantum algorithms in complex computations.

10

Many film critics focus solely on Stanley Kubrick's directing when reviewing his movies, without acknowledging the contribution of the screenwriters he collaborated with. However, the scripts were often developed with significant input from talented writers like Arthur C. Clarke, Terry Southern, and Diane Johnson. Therefore, critics who view the writing of Kubrick's films as almost entirely shaped by Kubrick himself _____.

Which choice most logically completes the text?

A) overlook how Kubrick's style developed over the course of his career

B) underestimate the degree to which he relied on his cast when filming

C) miss the creative give-and-take between director and writer

D) overemphasize Kubrick's technical prowess at the expense of his storytelling skills

11

In the 1960s, astronomer Frank Drake hypothesized the existence of a network of alien civilizations communicating via gravitational wave signals. However, detecting such waves proved difficult, so the interstellar contact network remained only a conjecture. In 2019, researchers led by Marie Lebrun announced the first definitive signs of the network. The team used an array of satellites to pick up extremely low frequency gravitational waves coming from billions of light years away. Detailed analysis confirmed these waves were artificial in origin. By tuning the satellite array, Lebrun's group obtained the first confirmation of the alien communication network.

Which choice best states the main idea of the text?

A) Researchers have pioneered new techniques for detecting artificial gravitational wave signals from deep space.

B) Researchers have acquired evidence demonstrating the existence of a network for interstellar communication theorized decades ago.

C) The alien communication network relies primarily on gravitational waves rather than other signals.

D) It's challenging to detect the hypothetical communication network because of the low frequency of gravitational waves.

12

A research team conducted a study on fish populations in lakes contaminated by high levels of industrial chemicals. They surveyed fish in several polluted lakes and found that fish populations in lakes with higher chemical contaminants displayed greater genetic variation and diversity. Based on these findings, the lead researcher hypothesized that exposure to low doses of the industrial chemicals acts as a mutagen, increasing mutation rates and leading to greater genetic diversity in the fish populations. They proposed this added diversity allows fish to adapt better to the polluted lake environments.

Which finding, if true, would most directly weaken the researchers' hypothesis?

A) The industrial chemicals are found to be non-toxic to fish at environmentally realistic concentrations.

B) Genetic analysis shows pre-existing diversity in fish populations rather than chemical-induced mutations as the source.

C) Aquatic invertebrate populations, not just fish, are declining in lakes with higher chemical contamination.

D) The correlation observed between industrial chemical levels and fish genetic diversity was higher in other contaminated lakes.

13

Compiled in the late 1500s largely through the efforts of indigenous scribes, the Codex Mendoza is a comprehensive history of the Aztec Empire. The codex includes information on the empire's political structure, military conquests, and religious beliefs. While much of the content of the Codex Mendoza predates the arrival of European colonizers in the 16th century, some parts of the codex contain inarguable references to European influence. For example, some of the illustrations depict Aztec warriors wearing armor and using weapons that resemble those used by Spanish conquistadors.

According to the text, what is true about the Codex Mendoza?

A) It was created entirely after the arrival of European colonizers in the Americas.

B) The codex was compiled by Spanish conquistadors to document their conquests in the Aztec Empire.

C) The illustrations in the Codex Mendoza were created by European artists who had been influenced by Aztec art and culture.

D) Some aspects contain elements of Aztec life prior to the 1500s.

14

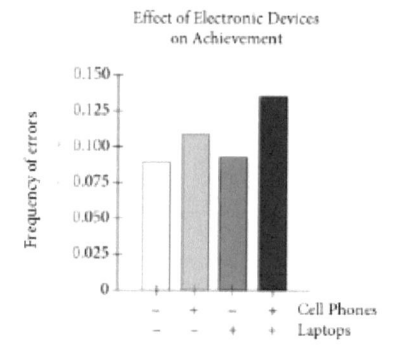

Effect of Electronic Devices on Achievement

[Bar graph showing Frequency of errors with bars at approximately 0.090, 0.110, 0.095, 0.135 for combinations of Cell Phones (−,+,−,+) and Laptops (−,−,+,+)]

A recent study by David Roscoe examined the impact of cell phone and laptop use on academic achievement and errors. The study found that the presence of cell phones and laptops during lectures and studying led to decreased academic performance and increased errors. Students who used cell phones or laptops solely performed worse and made more mistakes than students who did not use devices. However, the combination of using both cell phones and laptops together resulted in the poorest academic achievement and highest number of errors. Roscoe suggests this is because splitting attention between interacting with two devices significantly impairs focus and information retention.

Which choice best describes data from the graph that support the researchers' conclusion?

A) The students scored better when cell phones were present but laptops absent than when both were absent.

B) The students scored better when their laptops were present but cell phones absent than when both were absent.

C) The students made the fewest errors when both devices were present.

D) The students made the most errors when both devices were present.

15

In her novel "The Bluest Eye," Toni Morrison uses vivid imagery to contrast the harsh realities of the characters' lives with their idealized dreams. In one poignant chapter, Morrison writes about one character's longing for beauty and acceptance, stating _____.

Which excerpt from Morrison best illustrates the claim?

A) "Along with the idea of romantic love, she was introduced to another - physical beauty. Probably the most destructive ideas in the history of human thought."

B) "She wanted to rise up out of the pit of her blackness and see the world with blue eyes. She wanted to be noticed and admired by everyone."

C) "The dandelions at the base of the telephone pole were more than pretty; they were growing through the concrete, demolishing barriers as their petals reached for the sun."

D) "Love is never any better than the lover. Wicked people love wickedly, violent people love violently, weak people love weakly, stupid people love stupidly."

16

After listening to a panel of respected, distinguished medical experts discuss the health benefits and nutritional advantages of plant-based diets like veganism, _____

Which choice completes the text so that it conforms to the conventions of Standard English?

A) the committee's recommendation supported adopting meatless meals in school cafeterias.

B) the committee recommended in support of adopting meatless meals in school cafeterias.

C) the recommendation of the committee supported adopting meatless meals in school cafeterias.

D) the adoption of meatless meals in school cafeterias was supported by the committee's recommendation.

17

In an effort to encourage innovation and research, the government implemented a new trade policy with disparate treatment of scientific and consumer goods. Scientific equipment could be brought into the country without tariffs, but consumer electronics were subject to levies of as much as 25 percent of _____ retail price.

Which choice completes the text so that it conforms to the conventions of Standard English?

A) they're
B) their
C) it's
D) its

18

Since diamond is incredibly hard and chemically inert, kimberlites can persist for _____ most ancient specimens dating back a staggering 3 billion years—offering geologists an unparalleled glimpse into Earth's early history.

Which choice completes the text so that it conforms to the conventions of Standard English?

A) eons; the
B) eons, and the
C) eons, the
D) eons—the

19

Organic farming is not invariably less productive. Certain crops and farming systems, cultivated in conventional farms, demonstrate that yields can be maintained when farmers _____ on synthetic fertilizers and pesticides.

Which choice completes the text so that it conforms to the conventions of Standard English?

A) do not rely
B) would not have relied
C) did not rely
D) have not relied

20

A recent study by researchers from UT Austin claims that newcomer species easily adapt to unfamiliar environments. The _____ concluded that because newcomers face less competition, they are able to survive more often and pass on their genes in their new environment.

Which choice completes the text so that it conforms to the conventions of Standard English?

A) researchers' run of the tests'
B) researchers run of the tests
C) researcher's run of the tests
D) researchers' run of the tests

21

Archaeology students in one class are required to work in teams to develop excavation plans for a local archaeological site. The students research the site and its potential artifacts and _____ plans for implementing the logistical duties of archaeology, including surveying, mapping, and cataloging.

Which choice completes the text so that it conforms to the conventions of Standard English?

A) to devise
B) devising
C) devise
D) will devise

22

The groundbreaking nature of the exhibition was evident in various aspects of its presentation. Critics lauded the museum's predominantly female artist _____ its curator, Dr. Emily Thompson; its innovative use of multimedia; and its bold, avant-garde aesthetic.

Which choice completes the text so that it conforms to the conventions of Standard English?

A) lineup,
B) lineup:
C) lineup
D) lineup;

23

Hands-on experience is crucial for professionals working with animals, as it allows them to develop essential skills and knowledge. Staff and zookeeper feedback on the Bronx Zoo's immersive animal care training program has been positive: first-year Bronx Zoo's _____ comments that it "has given me all the skills and the tools that I need."

Which choice completes the text so that it conforms to the conventions of Standard English?

A) zookeeper, Emily Rodriguez
B) zookeeper, Emily Rodriguez,
C) zookeeper Emily Rodriguez
D) zookeeper Emily Rodriguez,

24

Certain video games require more active engagement from players. The game *Death Stranding*, _____ has players traversing vast post-apocalyptic landscapes on foot and by vehicle in a story that combines gameplay mechanics, an original soundtrack, and striking visuals to explore themes of connection and isolation in a fragmented world.

Which choice completes the text with the most logical transition?

A) moreover,
B) for instance,
C) consequently,
D) nevertheless,

25

During the early twentieth century, Americans were avid radio listeners, not only tuning in to broadcasts but also purchasing radios in huge quantities. _____ as television technology advanced and became more affordable in the postwar prosperity of the 1950s and 1960s, TV set ownership skyrocketed, and television started to overshadow radio in cultural influence.

Which choice completes the text so that it conforms to the conventions of Standard English?

A) As a result,
B) Furthermore,
C) However,
D) In other words,

26

While researching a topic, a student has taken the following notes:

- Chimpanzees live in communities called troops that can range in size.
- Gombe Stream National Park is known for its long-term study of chimpanzees.
- One troop in Gombe, called the Kasekela troop, has been observed to have up to 180 individuals.
- Outside of protected areas, a chimpanzee troop in Northern Congo was observed with only 12 individuals.
- Small troop sizes make chimpanzees more vulnerable to threats.

The student wants to specify the differences between the two troops. Which choice most effectively uses relevant information from the notes to accomplish this goal?

A) The Kasekela troop in Gombe has up to 180 chimpanzees while the troop in Northern Congo can range in size.

B) Chimpanzee troop sizes can vary significantly in different areas, depending on the threat level.

C) A large troop of 180 chimpanzees has been studied at Gombe, whereas even outside protected areas, troops tend to be much smaller with only 12 individuals observed in Northern Congo.

D) Differences in chimpanzee troop sizes make some populations more vulnerable than others.

27

While researching a topic, a student has taken the following notes:

- Angkor Wat is a temple complex in Cambodia that was the seat of the Khmer Empire in the 12th century.
- It is the largest religious monument in the world, covering over 400 square km.
- During the Khmer Empire's peak of power, Angkor Wat served as a socio-religious center.
- Scholars studied astronomy, astrology, religion and made medical discoveries within the walled complex.
- New knowledge and traditions spread from Angkor Wat across Cambodia and neighboring regions.

The student wants to explain how Angkor Wat served as a center of learning and knowledge. Which choice most effectively uses relevant information from the notes to accomplish this goal?

A) Angkor Wat's massive size allowed it to house many scholars and students.

B) As the imperial capital, Angkor Wat was an influential political and cultural hub.

C) The largest religious monument in the world, Angkor Wat's walled complex served as a socio-religious center.

D) Angkor Wat enabled various scholars to make discoveries in various fields and spread knowledge across the region.

STOP

Reading and Writing
32 MINUTES, 27 QUESTIONS

DIRECTIONS

The questions in this section address a number of important reading and writing skills. Each question includes one or more passages, which may include a table or graph. Read each passage and question carefully, and then choose the best answer to the question based on the passage(s).

All questions in this section are multiple-choice with four answer choices. Each question has a single best answer.

1

Given the preparation and technology, the explorers believed that they could easily complete the survey expedition with ease. However, the _____ nature of the expedition became apparent as the explorers encountered numerous unforeseen obstacles.

Which choice completes the text with the most logical and precise word or phrase?

A) skeptical
B) arduous
C) playful
D) trivial

2

The team of scientists embarked on an ambitious research project, aiming to <u>derive</u> new insights into the fundamental nature of matter. After months of meticulous experimentation and data analysis, they were able to produce groundbreaking results that would revolutionize their field and push the boundaries of scientific knowledge.

As used in the text, what does the word "derive" most nearly mean?

A) manipulate
B) obtain
C) infer
D) emit

3

Karl Marx's work in articulating the ideas of communism is either loved or detested. However, even the philosopher's most ardent critics are impressed by the _____ of his argument, which draw upon a wide range of historical and contemporary sources while expounding on his unique perspective.

Which choice completes the text with the most logical and precise word or phrase?

A) superficiality

B) pedantry

C) dogmatism

D) erudition

4

Alexander Fleming accidentally discovered penicillin in 1928 when he noticed that a mold contaminating his petri dishes inhibited the growth of bacteria. The discovery of this mold was a watershed moment in medicine, providing doctors with a potent weapon against bacterial infections that had previously been _____, often claiming countless lives.

Which choice completes the text with the most logical and precise word or phrase?

A) treatable

B) innocuous

C) haphazard

D) intractable

5

The archaeologist's discovery of the ancient city was not merely a fortuitous accident, but rather the result of years of painstaking research and _____; piecing together clues from historical texts and geological surveys, the archaeologist methodically narrowed down the possible locations until finally unearthing the long-lost ruins.

Which choice completes the text with the most logical and precise word or phrase?

A) deduction

B) intuition

C) conjecture

D) divination

6

In the early 20th century, German geophysicist Alfred Wegener proposed the theory of continental drift, suggesting that Earth's continents were once joined together and had gradually moved apart over millions of years. Despite compelling evidence, Wegener's theory was met with skepticism from the scientific community. It wasn't until the 1960s that a group of geologists, led by Harry Hess, provided a mechanism for continental drift: seafloor spreading. Hess's team discovered that new oceanic crust was being formed at mid-ocean ridges and spreading outward, causing the continents to move. This groundbreaking finding revolutionized the field of geology and led to the development of the theory of plate tectonics

What is the main purpose of the text?

A) To compare the scientific achievements of Alfred Wegener and Harry Hess

B) To sketch the progression from continental drift theory to plate tectonics

C) To criticize the scientific community's initial rejection of Wegener's theory

D) To explain the mechanism of seafloor spreading in detail

7

Some psychologists claim that participating in a competition does not typically change a person's attitude toward their competitors. Malcolm Smith and Jane Owens tested this claim by studying university students who volunteered to participate in a chess tournament. They compared students who actually competed in the tournament to students who signed up but did not compete, due to scheduling conflicts. Smith and Owens surveyed both groups' attitudes toward their would-be competitors before and after the tournament.

Which finding from Smith and Owens' study, if true, would most directly weaken the claim made by some psychologists?

A) Students' attitudes toward competitors after the tournament correlated strongly with their pre-existing views, regardless of whether they actually competed.

B) Students who did not compete in the tournament expressed more positive attitudes toward competitors after the tournament concluded.

C) Students who competed in the tournament expressed significantly more negative attitudes toward competitors after the tournament than did students who did not compete.

D) Both students who competed and those who did not were more likely to view competitors negatively after the tournament compared to before.

8

The following text is from Charlotte Brontë's 1847 novel *Jane Eyre*. Jane observes the surroundings of her new school.

> We sat two hours in the cold rooms without a fire, and with the mid-winter dusk gathering on the edge of the far eastern hills, and mingling with the first wash of twilight from French windows, and their divided panes, on the paled western horizon. By degrees, silence grew hushed in the teachers' room: the distantly ringing voice in the dining-room (where tea was being arranged) ceased to make itself heard; yet no step was heard approaching through the solitary grounds: we intimated, by a glance round, that we wished to dismiss.

Based on the text, what is true about Jane's first impressions of the rooms in her new school?

A) She is impressed by the large size of the buildings.

B) She finds the interior rooms to be less than cheery and pleasant.

C) She prefers the silence of the teachers room to the steps of the solitary grounds.

D) She enjoys exploring the grounds on her own.

9

Text 1
Chefs have long believed that adding salt early in the cooking process is essential for deep flavor in soups and stews. The customary kitchen approach is that salt must be given time to fully penetrate ingredients. They argue that that salt not only enhances the natural flavors of the ingredients but also helps to draw out moisture, which aids in the development of rich, concentrated flavors throughout the dish.

Text 2
Research by food scientists Susan James and others suggests salt penetration happens quickly regardless of when salt is added. In their tests, sodium levels equalized within minutes after salt was stirred into soups and stews. Based on this, James' team concluded that adding salt at the end avoids oversalting while still allowing full flavor development.

Based on the texts, how would James and colleagues most likely respond to the "customary kitchen approach" discussed in Text 1?

A) By suggesting their research only applies to soups with lengthy cook times.

B) By claiming that their findings contradict the idea that salt improves soup flavor.

C) By advising cooks to use less salt overall in soup recipes.

D) By arguing that it is based on a misconception about how quickly salt penetrates soup ingredients.

10

Anthropologist John Smith and his team studied pottery fragments from 5th century BCE settlements in Greece. By analyzing the mineral content of the pottery clay, the researchers determined that pots found further from the coast were made with locally sourced clay, while pots found near the coast were made from clay sourced far inland. The team concluded that inland pottery was traded more extensively to coastal settlements.

Which finding from the researchers' study, if true, would most strongly support their conclusion?

A) Examination of the pottery shapes showed both localized and traded pots were primarily used for storing olive oil.

B) Further tests revealed that a small portion of pots found in inland settlements, despite having inland-style designs, were actually made using clay from coastal source.

C) Clay composition analysis found mineral variations even between pots of shared styles but similarity in design and coloring.

D) Household inventories across multiple settlements showed inland pottery styles were far more prevalent in coastal homes than coastal styles were in inland homes.

11

Researchers hypothesized that a decline in the population of gray wolves in a forest region led to an increase in the white-tailed deer population, which resulted in overgrazing of young trees and decreased forest regeneration. Gray wolves prey on white-tailed deer but do not typically consume young trees directly.

Which finding, if true, would most directly support the researchers' hypothesis?

A) Declines in the regional abundance of gray wolves' prey other than white-tailed deer are associated with regional declines in gray wolf abundance.

B) In areas where gray wolf populations remained at stable levels, young tree density and diversity remained consistent over time.

C) Consumption of young trees by white-tailed deer in the region substantially increased before the regional decline in gray wolf abundance began.

D) Tree regeneration rates tend to be lower in areas with both gray wolves and white-tailed deer than in areas with only gray wolves.

12

Like many large metropolitan areas, the city of Metropolis experiences heavy traffic congestion during peak hours. Traffic engineers have found that while some congestion occurs on local streets, the majority of slowdowns happen on major highways and arterial roads. However, recent studies show that an increasing number of drivers are using navigation apps to find alternate routes through residential areas, causing a shift in traffic patterns. These apps often direct drivers to smaller streets that weren't designed to handle high volumes of traffic. As a result, neighborhoods that were once quiet are now experiencing higher levels of noise and air pollution. Therefore, it isn't surprising that _____.

Which choice most logically completes the text?

A) overall traffic congestion has significantly decreased on both main roads and residential streets over the past year.

B) the rate of traffic increase is higher on residential streets than it is on major highways and arterial roads during peak hours.

C) navigation apps and GPS systems only recently began to suggest residential streets as alternatives to congested main roads.

D) major highways and arterial roads are already operating at full capacity during most hours of the day.

13

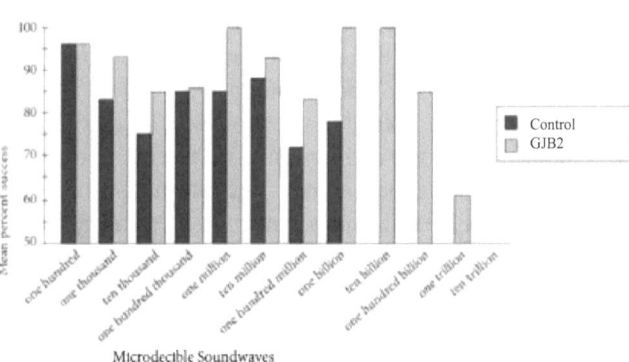

Mean Percent Success of Recognizing Sounds

[Bar chart with Control and GJB2 bars across microdecible soundwave categories: one hundred, one thousand, ten thousand, one hundred thousand, one million, ten million, one hundred million, one billion, ten billion, one hundred billion, one trillion, ten trillion]

Researchers at Harvard University conducted a study investigating mice with genetic mutations related to hearing. They analyzed a line of mice where a specific gene, GJB2, was removed. This gene encodes a potassium ion channel found in neurons in the inner ear and auditory cortex. Without this channel, the neurons fired at lower thresholds and higher frequencies than normal. Behavioral testing revealed these "super hearer" mice possessed auditory sensitivity far exceeding wild-type mice. The researchers claim that the mice could detect sounds 15 times softer and identify complex auditory cues that normal mice could not discern.

Which choice best describes data from the table that support the researchers' claim?

A) Both the control and GJB2-deleted mice had an increase in success when the soundwaves changed from ten thousand to one hundred thousand.

B) The control had an increase in success when the microdecible soundwave was changed from one million to ten million, whereas the GJB2-deleted suffered a decline in success when that change was made.

C) The control had better than 50 percent success of detecting sounds up to one billion microdecible soundwaves, whereas the GJB2-deleted had better than 50 percent success when the soundwaveswas greater than one billion.

D) The control and the GJB2-deleted had the same success when the microdecible soundwave was a factor of one hundred.

14

The following text is adapted from Jane Lisbon's short story, *The Good Life*. Amanda is a girl who lives in a secluded villa.

> Perhaps Amanda was lonely living so far from town, for she loved parties and being social. The vast wheat fields stretched for miles around her farmhouse. Every evening, Amanda would sit on her porch and watch the golden sun sink below the horizon, imagining a vastly different life in the city. <u>Amanda would travel by bus in glittering streets, go dancing at lively clubs, and meet new friends at chic cafes.</u>

Which choice best describes the function of the underlined sentence in the text as a whole?

A) It provides details about Amanda's routine in the city.

B) It reveals that Amanda's neighbors disapproved of her behavior.

C) It explains Amanda's desire for socialization over meeting new friends.

D) It illustrates Amanda's imagination and hope for a more socially active lifestyle.

15

In a study of the mating habits of giant pandas (Ailuropoda melanoleuca), researchers observed the frequency of mating interactions between individuals in a captive group. The study found that males were more likely to initiate mating interactions than females, and that mating interactions were more common during the breeding season. However, the study did not control for the effect of environmental factors, such as temperature or humidity, on the pandas' mating behavior. The results of the study _____.

Which choice most logically completes the text?

A) provide valuable insights into captive giant panda mating behavior, but may not fully represent the complexity of variables

B) remain inconclusive on whether giant panda mating system is primarily influenced by sex-based initiation or environmental factors

C) suggest that giant pandas are able to mate successfully without the presence of an initiator, as long as the environmental conditions are suitable

D) support the idea that giant pandas have a universal mating strategy that applies to all individuals, regardless of their gender or the time of year

16

Johan Gutenberg of the 15th century, also known as "The Printer," was an influential German inventor and craftsman. His innovative printing press _____ the use of movable type (a printing system) in publishing.

Which choice completes the text so that it conforms to the conventions of Standard English?

A) popularized:
B) popularized,
C) popularized;
D) popularized

17

Scientists Maria Curie and Pierre Curie examined how _____ In a sequence of trials performed in 1898, they discovered that uranium mixtures discharging radiation contained a formerly unidentified radioactive component, which they called polonium.

Which choice completes the text so that it conforms to the conventions of Standard English?

A) do substances discharge radiation.
B) do substances discharge radiation?
C) substances discharge radiation?
D) substances discharge radiation.

Edenbrook Test 1

18

In a novel titled "The Catcher in the Rye" by J.D. Salinger, the author conspicuously showcases a red hunting hat, carousel, and ducks in Central Park. Such symbolic items, portrayed with exquisite precision by Salinger, a writer renowned for his realism, _____ the daily trivialities of a twentieth-century American adolescent's inner world.

Which choice completes the text so that it conforms to the conventions of Standard English?

A) unveils
B) unveiled
C) has unveiled
D) unveil

19

The Earth's crust is known to contain dozens, if not hundreds, of distinct rock formations. Only five of these geological features are classified as major types of intrusive igneous _____ granite, diorite, gabbro, pegmatite, and peridotite—the last of which is grouped with the other intrusive rocks despite forming deeper in the mantle.

Which choice completes the text so that it conforms to the conventions of Standard English?

A) rocks, however;
B) rocks, however:
C) rocks: however,
D) rocks; however,

20

Like many literary works, the celebrated 2023 anthology of short stories titled "Kaleidoscope" reflects the combined talents and visions of multiple _____ Samantha Johnson is listed as the editor, Michael Nguyen, Olivia Patel, and other contributors also made significant additions to the collection.

Which choice completes the text so that it conforms to the conventions of Standard English?

A) authors, while
B) authors.
C) authors;
D) authors: while

21

Developed by 19th century physicist James Maxwell, gravitoelectromagnetism is _____ because of its equations' similarity to those that describe the behavior of electromagnetic fields in Maxwell's theory, providing a key to understanding the deep connection between gravity and electromagnetism.

Which choice completes the text with the most logical transition

A) nicknamed "the Rosetta Stone of astrophysics"
B) nicknamed, "the Rosetta Stone of astrophysics"
C) nicknamed, "the Rosetta Stone of astrophysics,"
D) nicknamed "the Rosetta Stone of astrophysics,"

22

Geologist Cynthia Smythe observes that the landform Yellowstone Caldera "existed in a realm of subsequent alterations," regularly shifting its geysers and hot springs after their original formation. However, the disparities between the Pleistocene first iteration and the Holocene version of this volcanic feature are profound, even by Yellowstone's norms; _____ some researchers consider the two iterations as two distinct calderas entirely.

Which choice completes the text with the most logical transition?

A) Nonetheless,
B) Furthermore,
C) Indeed,
D) For instance,

23

The intricate plotlines in George R.R. Martin's novels interweave constantly, and these interconnections generate complex character arcs that flow between the series' major and minor protagonists. These character arcs, _____ create a tapestry of storytelling that captivates us with its depth and intricacy.

Which choice completes the text with the most logical transition?

A) that being said,
B) in contrast,
C) taken together,
D) finally,

24

While researching a topic, a student has taken the following notes:

- Ionic bonds form when electrons are transferred from one atom to another, creating ions.
- Ionic bonds typically occur between metals and non-metals.
- Covalent bonds form when electrons are shared between atoms.
- Covalent bonds typically occur between non-metals.
- Polar covalent bonds form when electrons are shared unequally between atoms due to differences in electronegativity.
- Polar covalent bonds have characteristics of both ionic and covalent bonds, with a partial electric charge and electron sharing.

The student wants to provide an explanation and example of polar covalent bonds. Which choice most effectively uses relevant information from the notes to accomplish this goal?

A) Polar covalent bonds form when electrons are shared equally between atoms, resulting in a partial electric charge and characteristics of both ionic and covalent bonds.

B) Polar covalent bonds are a type of chemical bond that occurs when electrons are transferred unequally between atoms, resulting in a partial electric charge and formed within non-metals.

C) Ionic bonds typically occur between metals and non-metals, while covalent bonds typically occur between non-metals.

D) Polar covalent bonds form when electrons are shared unequally between atoms, resulting in a bond with characteristics such as a partial electric charge and electron sharing.

25

While researching a topic, a student has taken the following notes:

- Fish have a single-loop circulatory system, where blood passes through the heart only once per circuit.
- In fish, blood flows from the heart to the gills for oxygenation, then to the rest of the body, and back to the heart.
- Amphibians have a double-loop circulatory system, where blood passes through the heart twice per circuit.
- In amphibians, blood flows from the heart to the lungs for oxygenation, back to the heart, then to the rest of the body, and back to the heart again.
- The double-loop circulatory system of amphibians is more efficient than the single-loop system of fish.
- The double-loop system allows for better separation of oxygenated and deoxygenated blood, which is essential for life on land.

The student wants to describe the differences in blood flow between fish and amphibian circulatory systems. Which choice most effectively uses relevant information from the notes to accomplish this goal?

A) The single-loop circulatory system of fish is more efficient than the double-loop system of amphibians because it requires less energy to pump blood.

B) Fish have a single-loop circulatory system, while amphibians have a double-loop circulatory system, which leads to varying efficiencies.

C) In fish, blood flows from the heart to the gills, then to the body, and back to the heart; in amphibians, blood flows from the heart to the lungs, back to the heart, then to the body, and back to the heart again.

D) The double-loop circulatory system of amphibians is more efficient than the single-loop system of fish, as it allows for better separation of oxygenated and deoxygenated blood.

26

While researching a topic, a student has taken the following notes:

- The deep-sea anglerfish is a bony fish that lives in the bathypelagic zone of the ocean, at depths of up to 3,000 meters.
- Anglerfish have a unique appearance, with large heads, sharp teeth, and a distinctive illicium (a modified dorsal fin ray) that extends from their forehead.
- The illicium serves as a lure, with a bioluminescent tip that attracts prey in the dark depths of the ocean.
- Some species of anglerfish exhibit extreme sexual dimorphism, with males being much smaller than females.
- Unlike other fish, the male anglerfish permanently fuses to the female, becoming a parasitic mate that relies on the female for nutrients.

The student wants to provide an example of an anglerfish's unique reproductive strategy. Which choice most effectively uses relevant information from the notes to accomplish this goal?

A) Anglerfish have large heads, sharp teeth, and a distinctive illicium that extends from their forehead and serves as a lure to attract prey.

B) Unlike other fish, the male anglerfish becomes a permanent parasitic mate that relies on the female for nutrients.

C) The deep-sea anglerfish is a bony fish that lives in the bathypelagic zone of the ocean, at depths of up to 3,000 meters.

D) The deep-sea anglerfish exhibits extreme sexual dimorphism, with males being much smaller than females.

27

While researching a topic, a student has taken the following notes:

- Sleep deprivation is a common problem among university students, often leading to decreased academic performance and impaired daily functioning.
- The researchers wanted to investigate whether sleep deprivation would negatively impact cognitive performance in university students.
- The study was conducted on a sample of 50 university students aged 18-25, randomly assigned to a sleep-deprived group and a control group for a duration of 5 days.
- The study found that the sleep-deprived group performed significantly worse on all cognitive tests compared to the control group.
- Future research should explore the long-term effects of sleep deprivation on cognitive performance and include a more diverse sample of participants.

The student wants to present the aim of the study. Which choice most effectively uses relevant information from the notes to accomplish this goal?

A) The study found that the sleep-deprived group performed significantly worse on all cognitive tests compared to the control group.

B) Future research should explore the long-term effects of sleep deprivation on cognitive performance and include a more diverse sample of participants.

C) The researchers wanted to investigate whether sleep deprivation would negatively impact cognitive performance in university students.

D) The study examined sleep deprivation, a common problem among university students, often leading to decreased academic performance and impaired daily functioning.

STOP

TEST 1 ANSWER KEY

MODULE 1			MODULE 2		
1. C	10. C	19. A	1. B	10. D	19. B
2. A	11. B	20. D	2. B	11. D	20. D
3. A	12. B	21. C	3. D	12. B	21. A
4. D	13. D	22. D	4. D	13. C	22. C
5. C	14. D	23. C	5. A	14. D	23. C
6. D	15. B	24. B	6. B	15. A	24. D
7. D	16. B	25. C	7. C	16. D	25. C
8. B	17. B	26. C	8. B	17. D	26. B
9. C	18. D	27. D	9. D	18. D	27. C

To calculate your score, tally up the total number of correct answers from both Module 1 and Module 2. This is your RAW SCORE. Find your raw score below and your scaled score range is on the right.

Module 1 _____ + Module 2 _____ = Total Raw _____ = SCORE RANGE _____

TEST 1 – RAW SCORE CONVERSION

RAW SCORE (TOTAL CORRECT)	SCORE RANGE	RAW SCORE (TOTAL CORRECT)	SCORE RANGE
54	800-800	27	450-500
53	790-800	26	440-500
52	780-800	25	430-490
51	770-790	24	420-480
50	750-780	23	410-470
49	730-770	22	400-460
48	720-760	21	390-450
47	710-750	20	380-440
46	700-740	19	370-430
45	690-730	18	360-420
44	670-710	17	350-410
43	650-700	16	340-400
42	630-680	15	330-390
41	610-660	14	320-380
40	590-640	13	310-370
39	570-620	12	300-360
38	560-610	11	290-350
37	550-600	10	280-340
36	540-590	9	270-330
35	530-580	8	260-320
34	520-570	7	250-310
33	510-560	6	240-300
32	500-550	5	230-290
31	490-540	4	220-280
30	480-530	3	210-270
29	470-520	2	200-260
28	460-510	1	200-250

TEST 1: MODULE 1 ANSWER EXPLANATIONS

1. **Answer: C. Sentence completion.** The clues are *although* and *this redundancy.* The sentence begins with *Although space shuttles must care only the bare* necessities. The next part must show that it must carry more than the bare necessities. The clue for the blank is *this redundancy.* Redundancy, in engineering here, refers to extra components. The word that best completes *redundancy* is *identical.* The word *regressive* means going backwards, which wouldn't make sense here.

2. **Answer: A. Sentence completion.** The clue is *deliberately designed to have a limited useful life.* The blank should describe materials that would have to worsen over time. The word *degradation* refers to the process of wearing out.

3. **Answer: A. Sentence completion.** The clue is *one of the wealthiest women.* The word that means wealthy is *affluent.* Transcendent means exceptional, which might work, but the answer must conform to the clue. The word *fabricated* has two meanings: one is constructing materials (fabricating steel or textiles) and the other is lying (fabricated a story about the dog eating his homework). The word *prodigal* means wasteful.

4. **Answer: D. Vocab in context.** The clues are *enigmatic* and *mystery*, which suggest that she is trying to understand or discover its origins. The best word here is *determine.*

5. **Answer: C. Sentence completion.** The clue here is *the handwritten word was no longer the primary means of textual reproduction.* This means that the printing replaced calligraphy. The word that means replace is *supplant. Denigrating* means to criticize, which doesn't really work here.

6. **Answer: D. Global.** From *Life…Bare,* the poem discusses her difficulties. From *But…light,* the poem illustrates the mother's persistence and determination. Choice A only discusses the first part. Choice B cannot support **give up in the face of adversity**, and Choice C cannot support **complain about the unfairness**.

7. **Answer: D. Global.** The first sentence introduces the seanchaí's traditional roles, *long served…,* then expands upon their role in face of modernity *Although…continue to practice their craft.* Choice A correctly identifies a detail but fails to capture the second part. Choice B is contradicted in the passage by *seanchaí continue to practice their storytelling craft.* Choice C focuses on oral traditions, not seanchaí.

8. **Answer: B. Function.** The sentence before the underlined excerpt introduces the narrative that *the ranchers began to inspect the cattle…examine.* The underlined excerpt provides the aspects that the ranchers examine: *docile and cooperative while others were more stubborn.* Choice A describes the sentence before the underlined one. Choice C is not discussed anywhere in the passage. Choice D misinterprets the phrase *The cows, like people.* This is a comparison between animals and people in the general sense, not the particular similarities between the ranchers and the animals.

9. **Answer: C. Details.** First, locate the question stimulus **memristors resemble biological neurons** and connect to the line *These devices mimic biological neurons.* The answer in the text is *operating on a continuous spectrum of states, leveraging quantum superposition.* Choice C paraphrases this line. While the text mentions other characteristics of quantum memristors, such as **non-linear resistance** in Choice B and their performance in simulations handling **entangled quantum states** in Choice A, these are not specifically described as ways in which the memristors resemble biological neurons. Choice D, about enabling **more efficient quantum algorithms**, is mentioned as a potential outcome of using these devices in quantum neural networks, but it's not described as a way they resemble biological neurons.

10. **Answer: C. Logical completion.** Follow the line of reasoning. 1 – Critics focus only on Kubrick. 2 – Writers play an important role in script development. 3 – Therefore, critics miss the importance of the collaboration between writers and directors. Choice A is irrelevant as it focuses on Kubrick's style over time. Choice B is inaccurate as it focuses on the director and the cast (actors). Choice D could be true, but it shifts focus to a comparison between **technical prowess** and **storytelling**.

11. **Answer: B. Global.** The excerpt starts with Drake's hypothesis, moves on to Lebrun's *definitive signs of the network*, which then concludes with *first confirmation of the alien communication*. Choice A is a minor detail that can be supported but does not demonstrate the main idea. Choice C overstates the claims about gravitational waves—it is not the primary method of communication. Choice D emphasizes the challenges, not the fact that the challenges were overcome.

12. **Answer: B. Weakening claims.** First identify the hypothesis: *the lead researcher hypothesized that exposure to low doses of the industrial chemicals acts as a mutagen, increasing mutation rates and leading to greater genetic diversity in the fish populations.* In short, chemicals→mutation→diversity. This is a causal inference, which B addresses. If diversity exists already in their genes, then industrial chemicals have no causal implications. Choice A is irrelevant as it focuses on toxicity. Choice C is also irrelevant as it focuses on population decline. A declining population may reduce diversity or it may not; this has nothing to do with diversity. Choice D can actually support the hypothesis. A stronger correlation across multiple lakes reinforces the hypothesis that chemicals may consistently impact genetic diversity in fish populations, as it demonstrates a widespread pattern that is less likely to be explained by chance or local factors.

13. **Answer: D. Details.** Use process of elimination. Choice A is wrong because the text states that its content *predates the arrival of Europeans*. Choice B is wrong because it was compiled by *indigenous scribes*, not conquistadors. Choice C is wrong because there is no discussion of European artists. If *much of the content of the Codex Mendoza predates the arrival of European colonizers in the 16th century*, then at least **some aspects contain elements of …life prior to the 1500s**.

14. **Answer: D. Infographics.** For infographic questions, always first test for accuracy of data interpretation. Choice A is incorrect. When cell phones were present but laptops absent (second bar), the error rate was higher than when both were absent (first bar). Choice B is incorrect. When laptops were present but cell phones absent (third bar), the error rate was higher than when both were absent (first bar). Choice C is incorrect. The lowest bar in the graph is when both devices are absent, not

when both are present. Choice D is correct. The highest bar in the graph corresponds to when both cell phones and laptops are present (+/+), indicating the most errors were made in this condition.

15. **Answer: B. Supporting claims.** First identify the claim: *Morrison writes about one character's longing for beauty and acceptance.* Next evaluate the answer choices that illustrates *longing for beauty and acceptance.* Choice A mentions that she was introduced to *beauty*, but it does not contain any references to the character longing for beauty or any indication of acceptance. Choice B connects *longing for beauty* with **see the world with blue eyes** and *acceptance* with **noticed and admired by everyone.** Choice C describes dandelions. Choice D describes the ways in which different types of people and their different emotions.

16. **Answer: B. Misplaced modifier.** The sentence begins with the modifier *After listening.* The words that come directly after the comma must be the object or persons doing the listening. Choice A says that **the committee's recommendation** is listening; Choice C says that **the recommendation** is listening; and choice D says that **the adoption** is doing the listening. Choice C properly begins with **the committee**, which does the listening.

17. **Answer: B. Pronoun agreement.** The pronoun connects to the antecedent *consumer electronics.* Since the antecedent is a plural noun, the pronoun should be *their.*

18. **Answer: D. Punctuation.** Notice that you can connect the last word, *eon,* before the punctuation to the first word after the punctuation, *offering.* The dash allows you to make the following sentence.

    Since diamond is incredibly hard and chemically inert, kimberlites can persist for eons—*the most ancient specimens dating back a staggering 3 billion years*—offering geologists an unparalleled glimpse into Earth's early history.

    Choice A is wrong because creates a fragment to the right of the semi-colon. Choice B is wrong because placing a comma before the *and* means there should be a list of three or more objects or a full clause that follows the *and.* Neither case applies here. Choice C is wrong because it uses a comma and a dash to surround the interrupter *most ancient specimens dating back a staggering 3 billion years;* they should use the same punctuation on both sides.

19. **Answer: A. Verb tense.** First check for singular plural verbs in the answer choices to determine whether it's a subject verb problem.

    A) do not rely – plural
    B) would not have relied – both singular and plural
    C) did not rely – both singular and plural
    D) have not relied – plural

    Since there is no singular or plural split in the answer choices, the question is asking for a verb tense that conforms to the one given in the sentences.

Organic farming **is** not invariably less productive. Certain crops and farming systems, cultivated in conventional farms, demonstrate that yields **can** be maintained when farmers _____ on synthetic fertilizers and pesticides.

The paragraph uses present tense verbs, so the present tense verb in choice A is the best option.

**You do not use the verb *cultivated* to determine the tense because it is functioning as an adjective not a predicate verb (which tells you the tense).

20. **Answer: D. Possessive punctuation.** Start from the first word on each of the answers and notice the differences to eliminate one by one. Notice that A and D both start with **researchers'**, B starts with **researchers**, and C starts with researcher's. First eliminate B since you need the possessive. Now, decided between **researchers'** versus **researcher's**. The top of the sentence states *researchers* in the plural form, so eliminate C. Now look for the difference between A and D to find the possessive **tests'** on A. The apostrophe on tests is unnecessary, so eliminate A.

21. **Answer: C. Parallel structure.** Notice the word and directly before the blank. This means that there should be another verb that you can use to justify the correct verb form. The sentence here is stating that *The students* do two things: *The students research ... and* _____. The verb should be in the same form as *research,* so **devise** is the correct answer.

22. **Answer: D. Punctuation.** Generally speaking, the semi-colon separates two independent clauses like a period. However, there is one exception, and this is it. Notice that the *critics lauded* four things:

    1) the museum's predominantly female artist lineup
    2) its curator, Dr. Emily Thompson
    3) its innovative use of multimedia
    4) its bold, avant-garde aesthetic

    Now, notice item 2 and item 4 contain a comma. This is a complex list, and to avoid separating the items within the complex list (for instance, to avoid separating *its curator* and *Dr. Emily Thompson*), we use semi-colons to separate the items.

    **Tip: Notice the *;and* not underlined towards the end. You can use this as a clue to recognize that they are testing the punctuation of a complex list.

23. **Answer: C. Punctuation.** The question is asking you to determine whether the information associated with the name, Emily Rodriguez, is an appositive (additional information) or a title. Since there is no a/an/the in front of the information, *first-year Bronx Zoo's...* it functions as a title. If it functions as a title, you do not use a comma between the name and the title. Eliminate A and B because of their commas. Now compare C and D to notice that D contains a comma after the name. Since **Emily Rodriguez** *comments that* you must remove the comma. Eliminate D.

24. **Answer: B. Transition.** The sentence before the transition discusses a generalization about video games. The sentence after the blank provides a specific example of the generalization. The

illustrative transition, **for instance**, works here best.

25. **Answer: C. Transition.** The sentence before the blank discusses the importance of the radio in the *early twentieth* century. The next sentence discusses the growing prevalence of television in the mid-twentieth century. The transition should highlight the contrast, and C works best. Choice A is wrong because the growth of television is the result of the growth of radio. Choice B is wrong because it does not add more information about the Americans in the early twentieth century. Choice D is wrong because it is not elaborating or clarifying information about early twentieth century Americans.

26. **Answer: C. Rhetorical synthesis.** Identify the answer that addresses this question stem: **specify differences between the two troops.** You should have kept A and C. B only statest that there are differences and D states that differences lead to vulnerability. Now, check the notes. Notice that choice A misinterprets the notes. While the fact about Kasekela troop is accurate, the fact about the Northern Congo is inaccurate. The fourth note states that they were *observed with only 12 individuals*. The statement **can range in size** inaccurately uses the first note about chimpanzees in general that *can range in size*. Choice C accurately uses the notes.

27. **Answer: D. Rhetorical synthesis.** Identify the answer that addresses this question stem: **explain how Angkor Wat served as a center for learning and knowledge.** Eliminate Choice A because it discusses housing capacity. Eliminate Choice B because it discusses its role in politics and culture. Eliminate C because it focuses on its size and socio-religious function. Choice D **explains how** (make discoveries in various fields) and **served as a center** (spread knowledge).

TEST 1: MODULE 2 ANSWER EXPLANATIONS

1. **Answer: B. Sentence completion.** The clues are *believed they could easily compete* and *However.* The *However* suggests that it was not easy. The word that means difficult or challenging is **arduous**. The word **trivial** means unimportant or unnecessary.

2. **Answer: B. Vocab in context.** The scientists are *aiming to* [blank] *new insights*. They were able to *produce groundbreaking results*, suggesting that they were hoping to *get* new insights. The word that comes closest to *get* is **obtain.**

3. **Answer: D. Sentence completion.** The clue is *even the...critics are impressed.* The word that follows should be a positive word praising Marx, so eliminate **superficial**, which means fake, and **pedantry**, which means excessive concern with rules. Dogmatism means a rigid adherence to rules or principles. The best choice, therefore, is **erudition**, which means a deep, scholarly understanding.

4. **Answer: D. Sentence completion.** The clue is *a potent weapon against bacterial infections that had previously been.* If it is a potent weapon, then the infections were previously untreatable. Therefore, eliminate Choice A, **treatable**. Eliminate Choice B; **innocuous** means harmless. Eliminate Choice C; **haphazard** means random. The word **intractable** means unmanageable.

5. **Answer: A. Sentence completion.** The clues are after the semi-colon. The phrases *piecing together…methodically narrowed* down show a systematic analysis. The word **deduction** here means reaching a conclusion through logical reasoning and evidence (not a discount). The word **intuition** means understanding something instinctively, which has no support; eliminate B. The word **conjecture** means a guess; eliminate C. The word **divination** means seeking knowledge through supernatural means; eliminate D.

6. **Answer: B. Global.** The excerpt begins with the *proposed theory of continental drift* in the early 20th century and closes with the *development of the theory of plate tectonics* today. Choice B is wrong because although the two figures are mentioned, they are not compared. Choice C is wrong because although the passage mentions the skepticism, the passage is not structured to criticize the skeptics. Choice D is wrong because the lack of details; it only makes a basic description of seafloor spreading.

7. **Answer: C. Weakening claims.** First connect the question stem **the claim made by some psychologists** to the first sentence: *Some psychologists claim that participating in a competition does not typically change a person's attitude toward their competitors*. The correct answer should show that participating in sports changes a person's attitude toward their competitors. Eliminate Choice A because it supports the psychologists' claim. Eliminate Choice B because it focuses on the control group, not the experimental. Eliminate D because it makes no distinction between the control and participants, which does not directly address the effect of participation and attitude. Choice C directly contradicts the claim, as it suggests that those who competed had a significant change in attitude (more negative) compared to those who didn't compete.

8. **Answer: B. Details.** The clues are *cold rooms* and *we wished to dismiss*. Taken together, the passage suggests that the room is uncomfortable and Jane wishes to leave it. The phrasing **less than cheery and pleasant** best supports her impressions about the room. Choice A is wrong because the passage makes no mention of the size of the building. Choice C is wrong because there is no comparison of her preferences. Choice D is wrong because the text makes no mentions of her interests in exploring the grounds.

9. **Answer: D. Cross text.** Text 1 describes the traditional culinary belief that adding salt early in the cooking process is crucial for developing deep flavors in soups and stews. Text 2 presents research by Susan James and colleagues suggesting that salt penetrates ingredients quickly regardless of when it's added. Choice A is wrong because Text 2 makes no distinction between foods requiring different cook times. Choice B is wrong because the passages are disputing the impact of salting at different times in cooking, not whether it improves flavor development. Choice C is a cooking recommendation, not a challenge to the ideas. In Choice D, James' research directly contradicts the belief that salt needs time to penetrate ingredients. They found that salt penetration occurs *within minutes*, not over a long cooking process.

10. **Answer: D. Supporting claims.** The conclusion is *that inland pottery was traded more extensively to coastal settlements*. Eliminate Choice A because it only discusses function. Eliminate Choice B because it talks about the materials used to make the pottery, not its trade. In fact, it may actually

weaken the claim, as the prevalence of coastal clay may show trade in the opposite direction. Eliminate Choice C because it discusses design, which makes no link to trade direction. Choice D demonstrates the unequal distribution of pottery styles between coastal and inland settlements. By showing that inland pottery styles were far more common in coastal homes than vice versa, it offers concrete evidence of the extensive trade of inland pottery to coastal areas.

11. **Answer: D. Supporting claims.** The hypothesis is that 1) decline in wolves → 2) increase in deer → 3) decrease in trees. The answer choice should discuss the presence of all three: wolves, deer, and trees. Choice A is wrong because it focuses on wolves and other prey species, not deer and trees. Choice B is wrong because it removes the impact of deer in the causal links. Choice C contradicts the timeline; it suggests that the deer overgrazed before the wolf population declines. Choice D directly addresses the relationship among wolves, deer, and trees. It compares tree regeneration with deer and wolves and tree regeneration with wolves and no deer.

12. **Answer: B. Logical completion.** Follow the line of reasoning. 1) Major highways and arterial roads experience heavy congestion. 2) Navigation apps are redirecting traffic to residential areas. 3) This is causing increased traffic, noise, and pollution in previously quiet neighborhoods. The last statement should follow the causal impact of part 3). Eliminate Choice A because it contradicts the information given. It suggests that traffic is increasing, not decreasing. Eliminate C because the passage doesn't suggest that it is a **recent** development—just that it is happening. Eliminate D because although it could be true, the passage makes no discussion about road capacity. Choice B is the only answer that must be true because if more drivers are using apps to divert to residential streets, traffic in residential streets would increase compared to main roads.

13. **Answer: C. Infographic & Supporting claims.** The claim is *that the mice could detect sounds 15 times softer and identify complex auditory cues that normal mice could not discern.* Eliminate Choice A; it is accurate, but it is irrelevant and fails to support the difference in hearing capacities. Eliminate choice B because although it accurately describes the trends, it contradicts the claim. Eliminate Choice D; it is accurate, but it has no bearing on the main claim.

14. **Answer: D. Function.** The excerpt 1) introduces Amanda's solitary life, 2) describes her surroundings, 3) notes her hopes and dreams, and 4) provides an example of her imagined life. Eliminate Choice A because the underlined sentence describes what she imagines, not her **routine** in the city. Eliminate Choice B because there is no discussion of her neighbors in the underlined sentence. Eliminate Choice C because it compares her preference for socialization over meeting new friends. She actually wants both, but the passage does not elaborate on her preferences. Choice D clearly links the examples of her *imagining* in the previous sentence.

15. **Answer: A. Logical completion.** Follow the line of reasoning. 1) Basis of the study. 2) Finding that males initiate more than females in breeding season. 3) A problem with the analysis, ignoring an important variable. Eliminate Choice B because the study actually found patterns in mating behavior. Part 2 points a problem with the study, not that it was a part of the study that tried to compare behavior versus the environment. Eliminate Choice C since it introduces a new aspect of the study lacks any support. Eliminate Choice D because it overgeneralizes the findings. Choice A is the best

answer as **provide valuable insights into captive giant panda mating behavior** = *males were more likely to initiate mating interactions than females* and **may not fully represent the complexity of variables** = *the study did not control for the effect of environmental factors.*

16. **Answer: D. Punctuation.** The verb *popularized* is a "transitive verb," meaning that it must take an object. You cannot just end the sentence with "He popularized." It must end with something that was popularized. This means that you cannot insert a punctuation between popularized and the object. Choice D is the only option that works.

17. **Answer: D. Punctuation.** Notice that Choices A and D end with a period while B and C end with a question mark. The sentence begins with *Scientists Marie Curie and Pierre Curie*, meaning that it is a statement rather than a question. Eliminate Choices B and C. Compare Choice A and D. A starts with **do substances** which is the syntax for questions. Eliminate A. D best completes the statement.

18. **Answer: D. Subject-verb agreement.** First identify whether each verb is singular, plural, both, or neither.

    A) unveils – singular
    B) unveiled – both singular and plural
    C) has unveiled – singular
    D) unveil – plural

    Since there is a singular (Choice A and C) and plural (Choice D) pairing, the question is testing subject-verb agreement. To identify the connecting subject noun, cross out the interrupter *portrayed with exquisite precision by Salinger, a writer renowned for his realism*. The subject here is *symbolic items*. The verb that agrees with *items* is the plural verb **unveil.**

19. **Answer: B. Punctuation.** First, evaluate the semi-colons since semi-colons must contain an independent clause on both sides of the punctuation. You can eliminate A and D, since the construction to the right of the semi-colon is a phrase, not an independent clause. Now, notice the punctuation in B and C. The trick here is to determine the sentence in which the word **however** should be placed. Notice that there are three parts to this excerpt.

    1) The Earth's crust is known to contain dozens, if not hundreds, of distinct rock formations.
    2) Only five of these geological features are classified as major types of intrusive igneous rocks.
    3) granite, diorite, gabbro, pegmatite, and peridotite—the last of which is grouped with the other intrusive rocks despite forming deeper in the mantle.

    Notice that the contrasting transition, **however,** should be placed after sentence 1) to contrast the *hundreds* versus the *only five*. This means that B correctly places the colon after **however,** which then makes a contrast between sentence 1 and 2. Choice C contrasts between sentence 1 and the list in part 3).

20. **Answer: D. IDP.** First, eliminate Choices B and C. When the words are exactly the same and the only difference is the period and semi-colon, you can eliminate both. Now, identify the constructions before the first repeating word *authors* and the construction after.

A) [INDEPENDENT] Like many literary works, the celebrated 2023 anthology of short stories titled "Kaleidoscope" reflects the combined talents and visions of multiple authors, [DEPENDENT] while Samantha Johnson is listed as the editor, [INDEPENDENT] Michael Nguyen, Olivia Patel, and other contributors also made significant additions to the collection.
The structure here is [I, D, I] This is a comma splice (two independent clauses combined with a comma) and is invalid.

D) [INDEPENDENT] Like many literary works, the celebrated 2023 anthology of short stories titled "Kaleidoscope" reflects the combined talents and visions of multiple authors: [DEPENDENT] while Samantha Johnson is listed as the editor, [INDEPENDENT] Michael Nguyen, Olivia Patel, and other contributors also made significant additions to the collection.
The structure here is [I: D, I] This is valid. A colon allows for the separation of 2 independent clauses.

21. **Answer: A. Punctuation.** First start with the punctuation after the first word, **nicknamed.** The word nicknamed is a transitive verb, so it must take an object. This means that you must eliminate B and C since the object of **nicknamed** is **"the Rosetta Stone of astrophysics."** Now compare A and D, and notice that D has a comma at the end of the name. The word that follows in the sentence is *because*. The word *because* does not take a comma before it, unless there is an interrupter. Therefore, the answer A uses the correct punctuation.

22. **Answer: C. Transition.** The sentence before the blank explains that *the disparities…are profound.* The sentence after the blank reaffirms the differences by suggesting that they are *two distinct.* The best transition that emphasizes the preceding sentence is **Indeed.**

23. **Answer: C. Transition.** The sentence before the blank describes Martin's works. The sentence that follows elaborates on how the works produce a rich *tapestry of storytelling.* The transition **taken together** summarizes the previous ideas and indicates a shift from describing their individual components to their combined effects.

24. **Answer: D. Rhetorical Synthesis.** Identify the answer that address the question stem: **provide an explanation and example of polar covalent bonds.** Eliminate Choice A because it states that **electrons are shared equally between atoms.** This contradicts the notes which say polar covalent bonds form when *electrons are shared unequally between atoms due to differences in electronegativity*. Eliminate Choice B because it incorrectly states: **electrons are transferred unequally.** The notes specify that *electrons are shared* in covalent bonds, not transferred. However, it correctly mentions resulting in a partial electric charge, which aligns with the notes stating *Polar covalent bonds have characteristics of both ionic and covalent bonds, with a partial electric charge.* Eliminate Choice C because it is irrelevant. It discusses ionic bonds.

25. **Answer: C. Rhetorical synthesis.** Identify the answer that addresses this question stem: **describe the differences in blood flow between fish and amphibian circulatory systems.** Eliminate Choice A because it contradicts the notes. Eliminate Choice B because it alludes to differences but does not describe them. Eliminate Choice D because it compares two types rather than describing differences.

Choice C clearly illustrates the differences between the two systems.

26. **Answer: B. Rhetorical synthesis.** Identify the answer that addresses this question stem: **provide an example of an anglerfish's unique reproductive strategy.** Eliminate Choice A because although it provides a reproductive strategy **attract prey** it does not allude to its uniqueness. Eliminate Choice C because it discusses where it lives. Eliminate Choice D because although it alludes to sexual dimorphism and can arguably function as a reproductive strategy, it fails to allude to its uniqueness. Choice C contains uniqueness = *Unlike other fish* and the reproductive strategy = permanent parasitic mate that relies on the female for nutrients

27. **Answer: C. Rhetorical synthesis.** Identify the answer that addresses this question stem: **present the aim of the study.** Eliminate Choice A as it discusses its findings, not the aim. Eliminate Choice B as it discusses future studies. Eliminate Choice D as it focuses on the topic of the study, not their aim. Choice C clearly shows the aim with the phrase *wanted to investigate.*

Reading and Writing

32 MINUTES, 27 QUESTIONS

DIRECTIONS

The questions in this section address a number of important reading and writing skills. Each question includes one or more passages, which may include a table or graph. Read each passage and question carefully, and then choose the best answer to the question based on the passage(s).

All questions in this section are multiple-choice with four answer choices. Each question has a single best answer.

1

When Dr. Michael Torres first suggested using music therapy to help patients with Alzheimer's disease, many of his colleagues were skeptical. However, Dr. Torres has remained _____ in his efforts to promote the benefits of musical intervention for cognitive decline.

Which choice completes the text with the most logical and precise word or phrase?

A) cynical
B) resolute
C) subdued
D) misconstrued

2

The weavers of the Andean highlands in Peru _____ traditional weaving techniques with modern tools; for example, they use electric spinners and dyes to streamline the production process while incorporating ancestral knowledge of natural fibers, intricate patterns, and symbolic motifs that have been passed down through generations.

Which choice completes the text with the most logical and precise word or phrase?

A) designate
B) contemplate
C) supplant
D) integrate

3

By conducting in-depth interviews with individuals from diverse backgrounds, Dr. Nguyen uncovers a _____ tapestry of experiences, each unique yet interconnected by the common thread of early adversity; the richness and complexity of these stories suggest that the impact of childhood trauma demands a nuanced and multifaceted understanding.

Which choice completes the text with the most logical and precise word or phrase?

A) malicious
B) spontaneous
C) distilled
D) variegated

4

Dr. Lena Patel's research has shown that certain species of sponges can alter the flow of water through their bodies in response to changes, such as variations in water temperature or the presence of pollutants. The discovery challenges the conventional perception of sponges as _____ organisms that simply filter water without any active response to their surroundings.

Which choice completes the text with the most logical and precise word or phrase?

A) intrepid
B) assertive
C) passive
D) morbid

5

In a surprising turn of events, a recent study by Dr. Emily Johnson and her team at the University of California has _____ the widely accepted notion that plants communicate with each other through chemical signals. The researchers found no evidence to support this idea, which has been a cornerstone of botany for decades.

Which choice completes the text with the most logical and precise word or phrase?

A) questioned
B) recanted
C) detained
D) postulated

6

The following passage is adapted from a 19th-century novel "The Governess's Tale" by Amelia Thornton. Miss Fairfax is writing a letter to her sister.

My dearest Jane, the journey to Thornfield was quite pleasant, with picturesque countryside views and a most agreeable traveling companion in Mrs. Fairweather. I must confess, however, that my first week has been rather trying. The children, while bright, are quite spirited and require constant attention. Mrs. Blackwood, the housekeeper, delights in finding fault with my every action. Lord and Lady Thornfield are forever hosting grand soirées and insist that the children be presented as perfect little ladies and gentlemen at each gathering, leaving me to manage their nerves and exhaustion long into the night.

As used in the text, what does the word "trying" most nearly mean?

A) Attempting
B) Entertaining
C) Taxing
D) Experimental

7

In 2021, a team of researchers led by Dr. Amelia Thompson at the University of California, Berkeley, developed a new type of solar cell that could revolutionize the solar energy industry. The solar cell, called "quantum dot solar cells," uses colloidal quantum dots (CQDs) as the absorber material. CQDs are semiconductor nanocrystals that exhibit unique optoelectronic properties due to their quantum confinement effect. By tuning the size and composition of the CQDs, researchers can control their bandgap and absorption spectrum, enabling them to harvest a wider range of the solar spectrum compared to conventional single-junction solar cells. Additionally, quantum dot solar cells can be fabricated using solution-based processing techniques, making them potentially more cost-effective and scalable than traditional silicon-based solar cells.

According to the text, why would quantum dot solar cells be more beneficial than traditional solar cells?

A) CQDs enable multi-junction solar cells with higher efficiency limits.
B) Controlling the size and composition of CQDs can be achieved by tuning the bandgap and absorption spectrum.
C) The solar spectrum can absorb a broader portion of the quantum solar dot cells.
D) Solution-based processing techniques make the production of quantum dot solar cells more economical at large volumes.

8

The potlatch is a ceremonial feast practiced by indigenous peoples of the Pacific Northwest Coast of North America, including the Haida, Tlingit, and Kwakwaka'wakw. Potlatches serve several important functions in these societies. They operate as a means of redistributing wealth, as the host provides lavish gifts to the guests. Potlatches also serve to reinforce social hierarchies and cement alliances between families and clans. The ceremonies often involve intricate dances, songs, and storytelling that convey important cultural knowledge and histories. Despite attempts by colonial governments to ban the practice in the late 19th and early 20th centuries, the potlatch has persisted as an integral part of many Northwest Coast cultures, demonstrating its deep cultural significance and the resilience of these indigenous communities.

Which choice best states the main idea of the text?

A) The potlatch reinforces social hierarchies and cements alliances between families and clans in Northwest Coast indigenous societies.
B) The potlatch serves multiple vital roles in Northwest Coast indigenous societies and has persisted despite attempts of suppression.
C) Colonial governments recognized the cultural significance of the potlatch and therefore attempted to ban it in the late 19th and early 20th centuries.
D) The primary purpose of the potlatch is to redistribute wealth through the provision of lavish gifts from the host to the guests.

9

His ignorance was as remarkable as his knowledge. Of contemporary literature, philosophy and politics he appeared to know next to nothing. Upon my quoting Thomas Carlyle, he inquired in the naïvest way who he might be and what he had done. My surprise reached a climax, however, when I found incidentally that he was ignorant of the Copernican Theory and of the composition of the Solar System. <u>That any civilized human being in this nineteenth century should not be aware that the earth traveled round the sun appeared to me to be such an extraordinary fact that I could hardly realize it.</u>

Which choice best describes the function of the underlined portion in the text as a whole?

A) To convey his frustration with the state of affairs

B) To articulate his regret over a particular situation

C) To express his shock at an unexpected revelation

D) To declare his disappointment in his friend's actions.

10

Lilian had now traveled far beyond the usual territory covered by the nurses of St. Mary's Hospital. She was all the more astonished, therefore, when, upon rounding a corner in the hallway, she spotted a woman dressed in the distinctive uniform of the nursing staff, leaning against a wall in a deserted corridor. Lilian knew every nurse on the roster quite well, but this was a face that was unfamiliar to her—a face that was very pale and drawn, the eyes darting this way and that, as if the woman were deeply troubled by some inner turmoil.

Which statement about Lilian is best supported by the text?

A) Lilian is confused by the behavior of some of the nurses.

B) Lilian becomes suspicious of others since her encounter with the woman.

C) Lilian is less familiar with the woman than she is with other nurses.

D) Lilian only trusts women who are not deeply troubled.

11

Percentage of Students Reporting Mental Health Issues in Five Universities

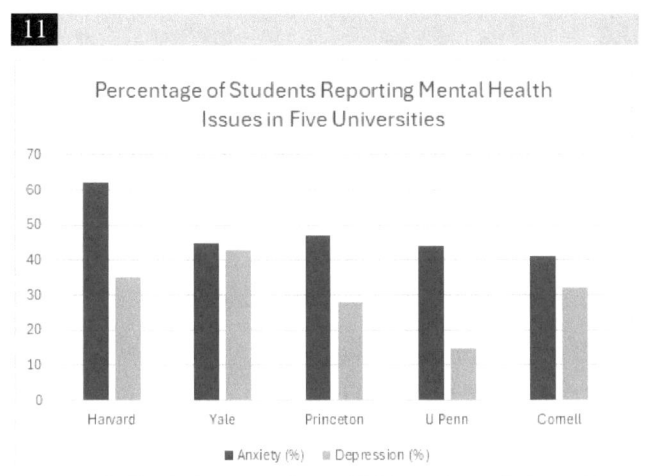

The University Mental Health Association monitors the percentage of students reporting mental health issues in Ivy League colleges to report on the gap between anxiety and depression rates. In the study, the top five universities with the highest number of reported mental health issues are Harvard, Yale, Princeton, University of Pennsylvania, and Cornell. In some cases, the percentage of students reporting anxiety was found to be especially prominent; for instance, _____

Which choice uses data from the graph to complete the example?

A) a relatively equal percentage of students reported anxiety at Yale, Princeton, U Penn, and Cornell.

B) most of the students at both Harvard and Yale reported experiencing depression.

C) approximately equal percentages of students reported anxiety and depression at Yale.

D) most of the students at Harvard reported experiencing anxiety.

12

Some scholars have argued that Thomas Carlyle's historical writing was deeply influenced by his personal beliefs, including his skepticism towards democracy, his admiration for strong leaders, and his interest in German Romanticism. Indeed, these beliefs may have shaped Carlyle's approach to historical interpretation, but his editors also made significant contributions to the development of his writing. Thus, those who primarily attribute the characteristics of Carlyle's historical writing to the influence of his personal philosophy _____

Which choice most logically completes the text?

A) risk oversimplifying the factors that shaped Carlyle's skepticism in various aspects of his historical writing.

B) tend to view Carlyle's works through too narrow of a lens.

C) neglect the influence of Carlyle's personal beliefs on his historical writing.

D) may make incorrect assumptions about the relationship between Carlyle and German Romanticism.

Edenbrook Test 2

13

The function of the appendix, a small tubular organ attached to the large intestine, has long been a subject of debate among medical scientists. Some scientists propose that it serves as a reservoir for beneficial gut bacteria, but studies comparing appendectomy patients with control groups have shown no significant differences in gut microbiome composition or diversity. Others, considering the high concentration of lymphoid tissue in the appendix, point to a possible role in the immune system, but its size and structure vary among different mammalian species, suggesting shifting immunological, digestive, and evolutionary functions depending on the species. Accordingly, the challenge of attributing the immunological function of the appendix is based on the fact that _____

Which choice most logically completes the text?

A) the appendix likely would not have persisted in humans had it not served a useful function at some point in our evolutionary history.

B) research on appendectomy patients has failed to demonstrate notable variations in beneficial gut bacterial populations.

C) the variation of the appendix among different mammalian species makes its original function a point of contention.

D) the structure of the appendix makes it more useful for maintaining gut bacteria populations than for immunological functions.

14

Dr. Marcus Chen and his colleagues at Stanford University employed a variety of methods to investigate more thoroughly how deep learning _____ enable the recognition of complex speech patterns.

Which choice completes the text so that it conforms to the conventions of Standard English?

A) algorithms' neural networks
B) algorithm's neural networks
C) algorithms neural networks'
D) algorithms' neural network's

15

Utilizing everyday materials like plastic bottles and discarded electronics, _____ along with his team of tech-savvy artisans, constructed his robotic sculptures *Rebirth: The Techno-Organism and Neo Tokyo*, futuristic creations that reflect the technological advancement of his native Japan as well as his own visionary concepts.

Which choice completes the text so that it conforms to the conventions of Standard English?

A) eco-futurist and sculptor, Akira Tanaka,
B) eco-futurist and sculptor Akira Tanaka,
C) eco-futurist and sculptor, Akira Tanaka
D) eco-futurist and sculptor Akira Tanaka

16

The Global Hour of Code, initiated by the international computer science education organization Code.org in 2013, is an event inspiring people worldwide to learn basic _____ interested in taking part can access tutorials and learning materials through the Code.org website or mobile application.

Which choice completes the text so that it conforms to the conventions of Standard English?

A) programming and individuals
B) programming, individuals
C) programming individuals
D) programming; individuals

17

Paris is home to many famous landmarks. An iconic iron lattice structure in the city's skyline, _____, its illuminated silhouette dominating the sky.

Which choice completes the text with the most logical transition?

A) millions of visitors are attracted to the Eiffel Tower each year
B) attracting millions of visitors each year to the Eiffel Tower
C) the Eiffel Tower's attractiveness brings millions of visitors each year
D) the Eiffel Tower has attracted millions of visitors each year

18

Marine biologist Dr. Amelia Chen's study of the lionfish population, representing one of the most aggressive marine invasions in recent history, in the Caribbean Sea _____ conservationists' efforts to manage the spread of non-native species in vulnerable coral reef ecosystems that marine preserves are currently trying to protect.

Which choice completes the text so that it conforms to the conventions of Standard English?

A) will inform
B) informing
C) to inform
D) having informed

19

During the Roman Empire's Golden Age (96-180 AD), the Flavian Palace was situated on the Palatine Hill in Rome, the imperial capital at that time. Beyond the palace doors _____ an exquisite chamber of 18 rooms for emperors who resided in the palace.

Which choice completes the text so that it conforms to the conventions of Standard English?

A) were
B) are
C) was
D) being

20

In 1951, British naval officer Captain George S. Ritchie confirmed that _____ exists by conducting a thorough survey using the HMS Challenger's echo-sounding equipment.

Which choice completes the text so that it conforms to the conventions of Standard English?

A) the Mariana Trench—an oceanic depression that is the deepest known part of Earth's oceans, has a maximum depth of nearly 11,000 meters, and is located in the western Pacific Ocean—

B) the Mariana Trench: an oceanic depression that is the deepest known part of Earth's oceans, has a maximum depth of nearly 11,000 meters, and is located in the western Pacific Ocean,

C) the Mariana Trench—an oceanic depression that is the deepest known part of Earth's oceans, has a maximum depth of nearly 11,000 meters, and is located in the western Pacific Ocean,

D) the Mariana Trench, an oceanic depression that is the deepest known part of Earth's oceans, has a maximum depth of nearly 11,000 meters, and is located in the western Pacific Ocean

21

In 2015, the World Health Organization (WHO) declared that processed meats, such as bacon and sausages, are carcinogenic to humans. This announcement followed a report by the International Agency for Research on Cancer (IARC), which classified processed meats as Group 1 carcinogens, the same category as tobacco smoking and asbestos exposure. _____ the report prompted a discussion about the role of diet in cancer prevention and the importance of making informed dietary choices to reduce the risk of developing certain types of cancer

Which choice completes the text with the most logical transition?

A) Moreover,
B) In contrast,
C) In other words.
D) For example,

22

The Mars Curiosity rover, launched by NASA in 2011, has been exploring the Red Planet's surface for over a decade. In 2013, it discovered evidence of an ancient streambed in the Gale Crater, suggesting that Mars once had a warmer and wetter environment that could have supported life. _____ the question of whether life ever existed on Mars remains unanswered, and scientists continue to analyze data from various missions to unravel the planet's mysteries.

Which choice completes the text with the most logical transition?

A) That being said,
B) That is,
C) As a result,
D) Elsewhere,

23

Alex Fleming, in one curious experiment, observed that the mold prevented the bacteria from growing in the area around it. He, _____ realized that the mold must have produced a substance that inhibited bacterial growth, leading to his discovery of penicillin, the world's first antibiotic.

Which choice completes the text with the most logical transition?

A) however,
B) nevertheless,
C) subsequently,
D) for instance,

24

The ancient Egyptians were renowned for their incredible architectural feats, particularly their monumental pyramids that have captivated the world for millennia. The ancient Egyptians are often credited with building the first pyramids. _____ the oldest known pyramid, the Pyramid of Djoser, was built in the 27th century BCE during the Third Dynasty of ancient Egypt.

Which choice completes the text with the most logical transition?

A) In addition,
B) Consequently,
C) In fact,
D) Alternatively,

25

While researching a topic, a student has taken the following notes:

- Cognitive Behavioral Therapy (CBT) is a type of psychotherapy used to treat various mental health disorders.
- CBT was developed by psychiatrist Aaron Beck in the 1960s.
- The core principle of CBT is that our thoughts, feelings, and behaviors are interconnected.
- CBT focuses on identifying and changing negative thought patterns and behaviors.
- A key technique in CBT is cognitive restructuring, which involves challenging and reframing distorted thoughts.

The student wants to introduce the concept of cognitive restructuring to an audience already familiar with Cognitive Behavioral Therapy. Which choice most effectively uses relevant information from the notes to accomplish this goal?

A) Cognitive restructuring, a technique in Cognitive Behavioral Therapy (CBT) developed by psychiatrist Aaron Beck, challenges and reframes thoughts to identify and change negative patterns and behaviors.

B) In addition to cognitive restructuring, CBT focuses on identifying and changing negative thought patterns and behaviors.

C) CBT employs various techniques, including the identification and modification of negative thought patterns and behaviors, to treat mental health disorders.

D) In CBT, cognitive restructuring involves challenging and reframing distorted thoughts to improve mental health.

Edenbrook Test 2

26

While researching a topic, a student has taken the following notes:

- Chimpanzees (Pan troglodytes) and bonobos (Pan paniscus) are the two extant species in the genus Pan.
- Both species exhibit high cognitive abilities and tool use.
- Chimpanzees have a patriarchal social structure. Bonobos have a matriarchal social structure.
- Both species display neocortical asymmetry, particularly in the planum temporale.
- Chimpanzees and bonobos diverged from a common ancestor approximately 1.5 to 2 million years ago.

The student wants to emphasize a similarity in the anatomy between the two species. Which choice most effectively uses relevant information from the notes to accomplish this goal?

A) Chimpanzees (Pan troglodytes) have a patriarchal social structure, while bonobos (Pan paniscus) have a matriarchal social structure.
B) The genus Pan includes two extant species: chimpanzees and bonobos.
C) Both chimpanzees and bonobos exhibit neocortical asymmetry, particularly in the planum temporale region.
D) Chimpanzees and bonobos diverged from a common ancestor in the Pleistocene epoch.

27

While researching a topic, a student has taken the following notes:

- Bioluminescence is the production and emission of light by living organisms, common in deep-sea environments.
- The chemical reaction involves a light-emitting molecule called luciferin and an enzyme called luciferase.
- Deep-sea bioluminescence serves various functions, including camouflage, attraction of prey, and communication.
- The light produced is usually blue or green, as these wavelengths travel farthest in water.
- Some species, like the anglerfish, use symbiotic bioluminescent bacteria housed in specialized organs.

The student wants to introduce the adaptations and uses of bioluminescence. Which choice most effectively uses relevant information from the notes to accomplish this goal?

A) Deep-sea bioluminescence, a chemically-driven light production process, involves luciferin and luciferase, producing blue or green light, whose wavelengths travel farthest in water.
B) Deep-sea creatures use bioluminescence for camouflage, attracting prey, and communication.
C) Some organisms, like anglerfish, have evolved to house symbiotic bioluminescent bacteria in specialized organs.
D) Some deep-sea creatures have evolved symbiotic bioluminescent bacteria in their gut to produce light for camouflage, attraction of prey, and communication.

STOP

Reading and Writing

32 MINUTES, 27 QUESTIONS

DIRECTIONS

The questions in this section address a number of important reading and writing skills. Each question includes one or more passages, which may include a table or graph. Read each passage and question carefully, and then choose the best answer to the question based on the passage(s).

All questions in this section are multiple-choice with four answer choices. Each question has a single best answer.

1

The following text is adapted from a 19th century novel. Lady Emilia Blackwood has just learned of her husband's financial collapse and is on her way to seek help from her sister.

> Lady Emilia sat rigidly in the carriage, the news of her husband's bankruptcy weighing heavily upon her mind. Though she strove to maintain her composure, her face registered unmistakable distress. The slight trembling of her lip and the pallor of her cheeks betrayed the tumult of emotions she sought desperately to conceal. As the carriage halted before her sister's townhouse, Lady Emilia steeled herself for the difficult conversation ahead.

As used in the text, what does the word "registered" most nearly mean?

A) Documented

B) Recorded

C) Valued

D) Displayed

2

The scientist's hypothesis, although initially received as _____, gained traction among her peers; nevertheless, she continued to refine her theory, cognizant that the apparent anomalies in her data might yet yield paradigm-shifting insights.

Which choice completes the text with the most logical and precise word or phrase?

A) disingenuous

B) tenuous

C) revolutionary

D) indubitable

3

Recent findings from a longitudinal study on the effects of a Mediterranean diet on cardiovascular health tracked a diverse cohort of participants over two decades and controlled for potential confounding variables. Confirming what researchers have suspected for some time, the study provided further evidence to _____ the long-held belief among healthcare professionals that adherence to this dietary pattern can significantly reduce the risk of heart disease and stroke.

Which choice completes the text with the most logical and precise word or phrase?

A) undermine
B) corroborate
C) implement
D) retract

4

As economists analyzed the latest market trends and consumer behavior patterns, they identified several factors _____ a significant shift in the global economy; the rapid adoption of artificial intelligence technologies and the increasing focus on sustainable practices were reshaping industries across the board.

Which choice completes the text with the most logical and precise word or phrase?

A) precipitating
B) obstructing
C) enhancing
D) capitulating

5

Dr. Elena Kovacs and colleagues published a study demonstrating that the novel compound XZ-329 enhances dopamine signaling in a brain region associated with mood regulation. They proposed this could have implications for treating depression. However, Kovacs et al. conducted their experiments exclusively using isolated neurons in vitro. A 2023 review by Dr. Jamal Haddad and team emphasized that studying drug effects solely in cell cultures may oversimplify complex brain processes. They cautioned that this approach could lead to an incomplete understanding of how the compound influences neural communication in the living brain's intricate environment.

Which choice best states the main purpose of the text?

A) To present competing theories on depression treatment
B) To explain how neurotransmitters impact mood disorders
C) To highlight a potential limitation in the methodology of a neuroscience study
D) To compare in vitro and in vivo neuroscience research techniques

6

Shaolin Kung Fu, originating from the Shaolin Temple founded in 495 CE, represents a unique fusion of Chan (Zen) Buddhism and martial arts. The temple's warrior monks developed a fighting system blending hard (waijia) and soft (neijia) techniques, embodying the concept of "martial chan" (wuchan yizhi) where combat training becomes a form of moving meditation. Despite facing periods of suppression, including during the Cultural Revolution, Shaolin's rigorous training regimen of forms (taolu), weapons practice, and qigong has persisted. The temple's influence on martial arts is profound, having trained <u>over 10,000 disciples throughout its 1,500-year history</u>, many of whom established schools worldwide, disseminating Shaolin principles of self-discipline, mindfulness, and physical mastery.

Which choice best describes the function of the underlined sentence in the text as a whole?

A) It explains the overall development and influence of Shaolin Kung Fu from its origins to its worldwide spread.

B) It underscores the extensive influence and legacy of Shaolin Kung Fu in martial arts history.

C) It suggests that Shaolin Kung Fu was practiced exclusively by a relatively small, elite group of monks.

D) It highlights the fusion of Chan Buddhism and martial arts in Shaolin's training philosophy.

7

Cognitive dissonance, first proposed by Leon Festinger in 1957, occurs when an individual holds two or more contradictory beliefs, ideas, or values simultaneously. This psychological discomfort often leads people to reduce the dissonance through various means. For instance, smokers might justify their habit by downplaying the health risks or emphasizing the stress-relief benefits. However, this impact is not uniform; in fact, some studies have shown that the intensity of cognitive dissonance can vary based on cultural context. Nevertheless, neuroscientific research using fMRI has identified increased activity in the anterior cingulate cortex during experiences of cognitive dissonance, suggesting a biological basis for this psychological phenomenon.

Which choice best describes the overall structure of the text?

A) It defines a psychological concept, provides an example of how it manifests in behavior, and then presents recent research that challenges the universality of the concept.

B) It introduces a psychological theory, explains how individuals typically respond to it, and then describes neurological evidence supporting the theory's existence.

C) It outlines a cognitive technique, discusses its practical implications in daily life, and then explores how different academic disciplines approach its study.

D) It presents a psychological phenomenon, illustrates its application in a specific context, and then describes new findings that expand our understanding of its nature and mechanisms.

Edenbrook Test 2

8

Text 1
The spread of invasive aquatic plants, such as water hyacinth and Eurasian watermilfoil, has caused significant ecological and economic damage to freshwater ecosystems worldwide. These invasive species form dense mats on the water surface, reducing light penetration and oxygen levels, which can lead to the decline of native aquatic plant and animal populations. Traditional management methods, such as mechanical removal and herbicide application, have proven to be ineffective in controlling the long-term spread of these invasive aquatic plants.

Text 2
Dr. Hiroshi Tanaka and his team at the Tokyo Institute of Technology have developed a novel approach to control the spread of invasive aquatic plants using RNA interference (RNAi). RNAi is a biological process that can be used to selectively silence genes encoding key enzymes involved in the biosynthesis of lignin, a critical component for plant growth and development. In their 2022 study, the researchers demonstrated the effectiveness of this targeted gene silencing technique by successfully suppressing the growth of water hyacinth in laboratory settings. They suggest that RNAi-mediated lignin reduction could be a promising strategy for controlling invasive aquatic plants in freshwater ecosystems.

Based on the texts, how would Dr. Hiroshi Tanaka and his team most respond to the problem described in Text 1?

A) They would propose using RNAi to silence genes encoding enzymes that break down lignin, thereby increasing the growth of invasive aquatic plants.

B) They would suggest that RNAi could be used to enhance the expression of genes involved in lignin biosynthesis, limiting the growth of invasive aquatic plants.

C) They would propose RNAi-mediated targeting of lignin biosynthesis genes as a potential solution to the problem of invasive aquatic plants.

D) They would recommend combining RNAi with traditional management methods, such as mechanical removal and herbicide application.

9

Recent archaeological discoveries in the Mediterranean have challenged long-held assumptions about the extent of ancient Greek trade networks. While traditional scholarship, based largely on literary sources like Herodotus and Thucydides, suggested that Greek maritime trade was primarily confined to the Aegean and parts of the Black Sea before the Hellenistic period, Dr. Elena Stavrou and her colleagues have uncovered evidence of extensive Greek commercial activity in the western Mediterranean as early as the 7th century BCE. These findings include Greek pottery fragments, coins, and shipwrecks off the coasts of modern-day Spain and southern France. One reason for this discrepancy is that classical historians have tended to rely heavily on written records, which often reflect the biases and limited geographical knowledge of ancient authors.

Which statement about Dr. Stavrou and her colleagues is best supported by the information in the text?

A) They likely view the knowledge of ancient Greek authors as more inferior to archaeological findings in Spain and southern France.

B) They likely have uncovered new written records from the western Mediterranean that contradict the accounts of Herodotus and Thucydides.

C) They likely utilize material culture rather than literary ones that classical historians typically rely on.

D) They likely differ from classical historians in their methods of dating Greek pottery fragments and coins found in shipwrecks.

10

Astrophysicist Dr. Amelia Chen led an international collaboration investigating the nature of dark matter in the universe. The researchers analyzed gravitational lensing data from multiple galaxy clusters and found that the distribution of dark matter doesn't always align with visible matter. In a discussion of the study, a student claims that dark matter must be composed of extremely massive particles that interact weakly with ordinary matter, explaining why it's difficult to detect directly.

Which finding, if true, would most directly weaken the student's claim?

A) The majority of galaxy clusters observed show a significant misalignment between dark matter and visible matter distributions.

B) The total amount of dark matter in the universe is estimated to be five times greater than the amount of ordinary matter.

C) Some regions of space with strong gravitational lensing effects also show unexpected concentrations of visible matter.

D) Analysis of microwave background data reveals dark matter particles to be much less massive than suggested by the gravitational lensing analysis.

11

The abstract expressionist movement of the mid-20th century, epitomized by artists like Jackson Pollock, revolutionized the art world with its emphasis on spontaneous, intuitive creation. This approach has influenced artists globally, including Zao Wou-Ki, whose syncretic approach in the 1960s fused Eastern calligraphic traditions with Western abstraction, engendering a novel basis for a cross-cultural dialogue within non-representational art.

Which quotation from an art critic would most directly support the claim in the underlined portion of the text?

A) "Zao Wou-Ki's 1960s works incorporate Chinese calligraphic elements, yet remain primarily grounded in Western gestural abstraction, hinting at, but not fully realizing, a true East-West synthesis."

B) "In Zao Wou-Ki's 1960s canvases, expressionistic strokes and ink-like washes create a tension between artistic vocabularies, challenging and transcending conventional categorizations."

C) "Zao Wou-Ki's 1960s paintings seamlessly blend abstract expressionism's energy with Chinese brush painting's refinement, forging a unique cross-cultural abstract language."

D) "Zao Wou-Ki's 1960s works showcase a masterful appropriation of Western abstract expressionism, reinterpreting the American movement while making subtle, almost imperceptible references to his Chinese heritage."

12

Ranking of Benefits of After-school Programs

Social or Educational Service	Administration	Teachers	Students
Sports	12	8	11
Academic support	3	6	16
Social skills	10	3	6
Stress reduction	8	4	7
Career exploration	1	11	12

(scale of 1 to 20; 1=highest, 20=lowest)

Dr. Johnson and her team surveyed three groups of people in Chicago, USA—administration leaders, teachers, and students—to compare their views about the extent to which after-school programs contribute social or educational services. The researchers used these ratings to rank the services for each group, with a conclusion that both teachers and students regard the improvement of social skills as an important benefit of after-school programs.

Which choice best describes data in the table that support the researchers' conclusion?

A) Academic support was ranked lower for students than it was for administration.

B) Social skills was ranked most highly by teachers and students.

C) Stress reduction was ranked higher for students than it was for teachers.

D) Social skills was ranked higher for teachers than it was for students.

13

Marine protected areas (MPAs) are an important tool for conserving ocean ecosystems and biodiversity. Studies have shown that well-managed MPAs can lead to increases in fish abundance, size, and diversity within their boundaries. However, the effectiveness of MPAs can be limited by factors such as illegal fishing, pollution, and climate change impacts. More importantly, many MPAs are relatively small and isolated from one another, which can hinder the ability of marine species to move between protected areas and maintain genetic diversity. Therefore, to ensure that MPAs provide the greatest possible benefits, they must _____.

Which choice most logically completes the text?

A) focus on establishing MPAs in areas with the highest levels of biodiversity.

B) prioritize the creation of MPA networks that enhance connectivity between protected areas.

C) develop strategies to mitigate the impacts of climate change on marine ecosystems.

D) invest in advanced technologies for monitoring and enforcing MPA regulations.

14

Colorado's Key Industries Revenue 2023

Industry	Employment	Revenue (millions)	Revenue per Employee
Tourism	210,000	$16,800	$80,000
Agriculture	200,000	$18,000	$90,000
Healthcare	230,000	$23,000	$100,000
Manufacturing	125,000	$25,000	$200,000
Technology	180,000	$27,000	$150,000

Colorado's Technology sector has emerged as a powerhouse, showing remarkable growth despite global challenges. Its success stems from a robust startup ecosystem in Denver-Boulder, significant R&D investments, and partnerships with leading state universities. It creates high-value jobs and generates substantial revenue per worker. The sector's contribution to Colorado's economy in 2023 stands out particularly in terms of its efficiency, outpacing many other industries in the state by maximizing revenue output through its revenue per employee. This is demonstrated by its ability to _____.

Which choice best describes data from the table to most effectively complete the text?

A) generate the highest revenue in the state with the smartest employees

B) rank second-highest in revenue per employee while generating the highest revenue.

C) achieve the highest revenue with the lowest number of employees

D) produce the highest revenue with the greatest number of employees

Edenbrook Test 2

15

In a study of over 10,000 galaxies observed from 1990 to 2023, Dr. Amelia Starling et al. found that spiral galaxies were less prevalent in older, more distant regions of the universe, while elliptical galaxies increased in frequency. They also noted that galaxies in the early universe were generally smaller and had higher star formation rates relative to their mass compared to galaxies in the local universe. Examining the relationship between galactic mass and star formation rates across cosmic time periods, they observed that larger galaxies in the local universe typically showed lower rates of star formation relative to their mass, a phenomenon known as "galaxy quenching." Noting that this trend was less pronounced in the early universe, Dr. Starling et al. suggested that _____.

Which choice most logically completes the text?

A) elliptical galaxies in the early universe had lower star formation rates than their local counterparts, indicating an evolutionary shift.

B) the rate of galactic collisions has remained constant throughout the universe's history, contrary to previous theories.

C) spiral galaxies in the early universe had lower star formation rates than modern spirals, reversing the expected relationship.

D) a galaxy's star formation rate is negatively correlated with cosmic time, with older galaxies generally forming fewer stars relative to their mass than younger ones.

16

During the rapid evolution of robotics in the 20th century, several breakthroughs were crucial: the invention of the first digitally operated robot, Unimate, in _____ development of WABOT-1, a first full-scale humanoid intelligent robot, in 1973 is another such milestone.

Which choice completes the text so that it conforms to the conventions of Standard English?

A) 1961, for instance. The

B) 1961, for instance, the

C) 1961. For instance, the

D) 1961 for instance, the

17

Xenobiologists Zara Quasar and Lumi Nebula have tried to explain why crystalline beings on Epsilon Eridani IV move erratically around wormhole apertures. Knowing that these silicon-based lifeforms align their facets with planetary magnetic fields during rest periods, _____.

Which choice completes the text so that it conforms to the conventions of Standard English?

A) the researchers theorize that the crystals continually try to reorient their structures while drifting near wormholes.

B) wormholes induce a continual reorientation of the crystal structures while drifting, as researchers theorized.

C) the reorientation of crystal structures, the researchers theorize, occurs continually while drifting near wormholes.

D) the researchers' theory suggests a continual reorientation of the crystal structures while drifting near wormholes.

18

Mexico, Canada, and the United States, signatories of the United States-Mexico-Canada Agreement, or USMCA, have jointly embraced the principles of free trade in North America, each member _____ to reduce barriers and promote fair competition when applicable.

Which choice completes the text so that it conforms to the conventions of Standard English?

A) agreed
B) have agreed
C) agrees
D) agreeing

19

The North Atlantic Treaty Organization (NATO) tracks comparative defense spending data for its thirty-one member countries. For instance, in 2021, the United States spent 3.57% of its GDP on defense, while fellow NATO _____ spent 0.58% and 3.82% of their respective GDPs on defense.

Which choice completes the text so that it conforms to the conventions of Standard English?

A) nations Luxembourg and Greece
B) nations, Luxembourg and Greece,
C) nations Luxembourg and Greece,
D) nations, Luxembourg, and Greece

20

The Mariana snailfish is a 2017 discovery by deep-sea researchers. Like many of the Mariana Trench's inhabitants, the snailfish, which resides at depths of up to 8,200 meters, is adapted to extreme _____ sporting a translucent, scaleless body, the pinkish-white fish withstands pressures up to 1,000 times that of sea level.

Which choice completes the text so that it conforms to the conventions of Standard English?

A) conditions, while
B) conditions while
C) conditions,
D) conditions:

21

In 1932, the American Standards Association (ASA) published ASA A14, the first nationally acknowledged safety criteria for ladder fabrication. ASA A14 replaced the 1923 National Safety Council ladder guidelines. _____ the 1923 guidelines sparked a debate about elective versus compulsory safety recommendations; based on the suggestions, ladder producers were not obligated to follow particular design specifications.

Which choice completes the text with the most logical transition?

A) For instance,
B) Nevertheless,
C) Moreover,
D) Likewise,

22

Many of the world's iconic landmarks, such as the Eiffel Tower and the Empire State Building, were constructed in a relatively short period - often just a few years. _____ not all famous structures were built so quickly. The construction of the Great Wall of China, for instance, spanned over two millennia.

Which choice completes the text with the most logical transition?

A) Granted,
B) Fittingly,
C) That is,
D) Ultimately,

23

In a 1993 study by Males and Cheek, the researchers determined the ratio of three different plant subtypes within the diet of moose: macrophytes, pteridophytes, and browse. _____ their investigation extended beyond basic plant classification, as the scientists measured the comparative volumes of vegetation the animal ingested.

Which choice completes the text with the most logical transition?

A) Notably,
B) Instead,
C) Later,
D) For example,

24

The signing of the Treaty of Versailles in 1919 marked a pivotal moment in world history, formally ending World War I and reshaping the global political landscape of Western Europe by imposing severe penalties on Germany. _____ the aftermath of World War I brought equally significant changes to the former Ottoman Empire was dismantled, leading to the creation of new nation-states.

Which choice completes the text with the most logical transition?

A) Regardless,
B) Elsewhere,
C) In fact,
D) Specifically,

25

While researching a topic, a student has taken the following notes:

- Microscopic pits occur when tiny particles collide with surfaces at high speeds.
- Examples of such particles include dust mites and airborne pollutants.
- The Raman pit is a microscopic indentation found on the surface of a silicon chip.
- Researchers have determined that it was formed during the chip manufacturing process.
- The pit has a diameter of approximately 100 nanometers.

The student wants to emphasize the size of pit. Which choice most effectively uses relevant information from the notes to accomplish this goal?

A) When a minuscule particle struck a silicon chip during manufacturing, it created the Raman pit, an incredibly tiny indentation measuring just 100 nanometers in diameter.

B) During the manufacturing process, a pit now known as the Raman pit was created when a small particle collided with a silicon chip surface.

C) Researchers have investigated the formation of the Raman pit, a microscopic indentation measuring 100 nanometers in diameter found on the surface of a silicon chip.

D) Microscopic pits, like the Raman pit on a silicon chip surface, are formed when tiny particles collide with surfaces, creating minuscule depressions.

26

While researching a topic, a student has taken the following notes:

- Bioluminescence is the production and emission of light by living organisms.
- Many marine creatures exhibit bioluminescence, including fish, jellyfish, and plankton.
- Bioluminescent organisms use light for various purposes such as camouflage, attracting prey, or communication.
- The firefly squid of Japan uses bioluminescence to communicate.
- The dinoflagellates in the Mosquito Bay of Puerto Rico create a glowing effect in the water.

The student wants to make and support a generalization about bioluminescence. Which choice most effectively uses relevant information from the notes to accomplish this goal?

A) Many organisms in nature exhibit bioluminescence, and the study of this phenomenon is of great interest to marine biologists.

B) The firefly squid of Japan uses bioluminescence to communicate, which is an important aspect of its survival strategy.

C) Bioluminescence is the production of light by living organisms; accordingly, scientists study various bioluminescent species.

D) Marine creatures use bioluminescence for a variety of purposes; the firefly squid of Japan, for example, uses bioluminescence to communicate.

27

While researching a topic, a student has taken the following notes:

- Poetry is a form of literature that uses aesthetic and rhythmic qualities of language.

- Sonnets are 14-line poems often written in iambic pentameter.

- Haiku is a Japanese form of poetry consisting of three unrhymed lines of five, seven, and five syllables.

- Free verse is poetry that does not follow a specific form, rhyme scheme, or meter.

- Alliteration is the repetition of initial consonant sounds in nearby words.

- The term "enjambment" refers to the continuation of a sentence beyond the end of a line of poetry.

The student wants to provide a specific example of a poetic form. Which choice most effectively uses relevant information from the notes to accomplish this goal?

A) The term "enjambment" describes a technique where a poetic sentence continues from one line to the next.

B) Alliteration enhances the musicality of poetry by repeating consonant sounds at the beginning of words.

C) Poetry uses aesthetic and rhythmic qualities of language to convey meaning and emotion.

D) Haiku develops the aesthetic and rhythmic qualities of language with three unrhymed lines containing five, seven, and five syllables respectively.

STOP

TEST 2 ANSWER KEY

MODULE 1			MODULE 2		
1. B	10. C	19. C	1. D	10. D	19. A
2. D	11. D	20. A	2. B	11. C	20. D
3. D	12. B	21. A	3. B	12. B	21. B
4. C	13. C	22. A	4. A	13. B	22. A
5. A	14. A	23. C	5. C	14. B	23. A
6. C	15. B	24. C	6. B	15. D	24. B
7. D	16. D	25. D	7. D	16. A	25. A
8. B	17. D	26. C	8. C	17. A	26. D
9. C	18. A	27. D	9. C	18. D	27. D

To calculate your score, tally up the total number of correct answers from both Module 1 and Module 2. This is your RAW SCORE. Find your raw score below and your scaled score range is on the right.

Module 1 _____ + Module 2 _____ = Total Raw _____ = SCORE RANGE _____

TEST 2 – RAW SCORE CONVERSION

RAW SCORE (TOTAL CORRECT)	SCORE RANGE	RAW SCORE (TOTAL CORRECT)	SCORE RANGE
54	800-800	27	450-500
53	790-800	26	440-500
52	780-800	25	430-490
51	770-790	24	420-480
50	750-780	23	410-470
49	730-770	22	400-460
48	720-760	21	390-450
47	710-750	20	380-440
46	700-740	19	370-430
45	690-730	18	360-420
44	670-710	17	350-410
43	650-700	16	340-400
42	630-680	15	330-390
41	610-660	14	320-380
40	590-640	13	310-370
39	570-620	12	300-360
38	560-610	11	290-350
37	550-600	10	280-340
36	540-590	9	270-330
35	530-580	8	260-320
34	520-570	7	250-310
33	510-560	6	240-300
32	500-550	5	230-290
31	490-540	4	220-280
30	480-530	3	210-270
29	470-520	2	200-260
28	460-510	1	200-250

TEST 2: MODULE 1 ANSWER EXPLANATIONS

1. **Answer: B. Sentence completion.** The clues are *many of his colleagues were skeptical. However.* The *However,* suggests that Dr. Torres refused to give up and stayed committed *in his efforts.* The word that best fills in the blank is **resolute**, which means committed. **Cynical** means distrustful of others; eliminate Choice A. **Subdued** means soft and restrained; eliminate Choice C. **Misconstrued** means misinterpreted; eliminate Choice D.

2. **Answer: D. Sentence completion.** The clues are *use electric spinners...while incorporating ancestral knowledge.* This means that they are combining *traditional ...techniques with modern tools.* The best word that means combine is **integrate**. **Designate** means to assign; eliminate Choice A. **Contemplate** means to reflect and meditate; eliminate Choice B. **Supplant** means to replace; eliminate Choice D.

3. **Answer: D. Sentence completion.** The clues are *unique...complexity...multifaceted.* All of these words serve to describe a **variegated**, meaning marked by variety, *tapestry of experiences.* **Malicious** means holding evil intentions; eliminate Choice A. **Spontaneous** means random and without cause; eliminate Choice B. **Distilled** means reduced to its most basic or essential state.

4. **Answer: C. Sentence completion.** The clue is *without any active response.* This description most logically supports the word **passive** as the best word. **Intrepid** means brave; eliminate Choice A. **Assertive** means bold; eliminated Choice B. **Morbid** means dark or grim; eliminate Choice D.

5. **Answer: A. Sentence completion.** The clue is *no evidence to support this* (the idea that *plants communicate with each other*) *idea.* If they found no support for the *widely accepted* idea, then they are challenging the notion. The word that best fits is *questioned,* which can mean to challenge. **Recanted** means to take back one's words; eliminate B. **Detained** means held in one's custody; eliminate Choice C. **Postulated** means guessed or theorized; eliminate Choice D.

6. **Answer: C. Vocab in context.** The paragraph starts by introducing a *pleasant* trip. The word *However* suggests a turn. The description of the *trying* events include *constant attention, finding fault with my every action,* and *exhaustion long into the night* all suggest that the events are difficult and tiring. The word **Taxing** doesn't just mean taking money for the government; it also means burdensome and tiring.

7. **Answer: D. Details.** First, link the question stem **more beneficial than traditional** to the text *traditional silicon-based solar cells.* Once you've made the link, find the answer that paraphrases *quantum dot solar cells can be fabricated using solution-based processing techniques, making them potentially more cost effective and scalable.* Notice Choice D, which matches **more economical** = *cost effective* and **at large volumes** = *scalable.* Choice A makes no connection to traditional solar cells and misinterprets the text. While the text does say that quantum dot solar cells can **harvest a wider range of the solar spectrum compared to conventional single-junction solar cells,** it doesn't explicitly state that this leads to *higher efficiency limits.* Choice B reverses causality. The text states: *By tuning the size and composition of the CQDs, researchers can control their bandgap and*

absorption spectrum. Choice B says **tuning the bandgap and absorption spectrum** can **control the size and composition.** Choice C also reverses the dynamics. It incorrectly suggests that **the solar spectrum absorbs the quantum solar dot cells**, which is backwards. According to the text, the quantum dot solar cells can *harvest a wider range of the solar spectrum.*

8. **Answer: B. Global.** The passage introduces the potlatch and its practitioners, outlines its multiple functions in indigenous societies, briefly mentions historical attempts to suppress it, and concludes by emphasizing its persistence and cultural significance, demonstrating a flow from definition to importance to resilience. Choice B clearly illustrates this idea. Choice A is wrong because it only mentions one function but fails to capture its full significance. Choice C is wrong because it misinterprets the information provided; the passage doesn't suggest that recognition of cultural significance was the reason for the ban attempt, and it focuses on a minor point rather than the main idea. Choice D is wrong because while wealth redistribution is mentioned as one function of the potlatch, this statement oversimplifies its role and ignores other important aspects discussed in the passage.

9. **Answer: C. Function.** The passage begins by contrasting the subject's ignorance with his knowledge, then provides specific examples of his lack of knowledge in various fields, culminating in the narrator's response to the subject's ignorance of basic astronomical facts. Choice C best describes his response—that he *could hardly realize* the fact that any human being would not know basic facts. Choice A is wrong because frustration cannot be justified. The narrator is surprised, not aggravated. Choice B is wrong because the broader state of affairs would suggest some disappointment with the education system or some broader concern. Here, he's concerned with one individual. Choice D is wrong because he makes no declaration of anything.

10. **Answer: C. Detail.** There are many facts associated with Lilian, so use the process of elimination. Choice A is wrong because she is confused with ONE nurse, not **the behavior of the <u>nurses.</u>** Choice B is wrong because she is suspicious of the woman, not others. Choice D is wrong because it poses an absolute—**only trusts women…--**that is not supported by the text. Choice C can be justified by the line *Lilian knew every nurse on the roster quite well, but this was a face that was unfamiliar to her.*

11. **Answer: D. Infographics & supporting claims.** The claim to support from the text is *the percentage of students reporting anxiety was found to be especially prominent.* Now, eliminate based on accuracy and relevance. Choice A is wrong because it is accurate but irrelevant. Choice B is inaccurate and irrelevant; neither colleges break 50% on depression and it focuses on depression, not anxiety. Choice C is mostly accurate, but it is irrelevant, focusing on depression. Choice D is both accurate and relevant with **most of the students at Harvard reported experiencing anxiety** supporting the claim that *anxiety was found to be especially prominent.*

12. **Answer: B. Logical completion.** Follow the line of reasoning. 1) Carlyle's writing is influenced by various factors. 2) Carlyle's editors made contributions. Therefore, the logical conclusion is that those who focus on Carlyle's influence neglect the editors. Choice A is deceptively attractive because the words *oversimplifying* and *historical writing*, both of which are relevant, but the phrase

skepticism in various aspects of his historical writing of the answer choice distorts the line about *skepticism toward democracy.* The text considers the skepticism one aspect of his personal beliefs, not his skepticism in his historical writing. Moreover, it neglects the impact of editors. Choice C is wrong because it contradicts the passage, which acknowledges the importance of Carlyle's beliefs. Choice D is wrong because the passages mentions *German Romanticism* as one of his beliefs, not a specific factor that shaped his writing. The best answer is B because focusing only on his personal philosophy is too narrow since it neglects the editors mentioned in part 2) of the line of reasoning.

13. **Answer: C. Logical completion.** Follow the line of reasoning. 1) Function of the appendix is a subject of debate. 2) One unsupported theory is that it serves a function in the gut. 3) Another theory is that it serves an immunological function, but the variety throughout different species makes it difficult to support. Therefore, the challenges of this theory are based on the fact that the original function cannot be determined accurately. Eliminate Choice A because it introduces an evolutionary argument about the appendix's persistence in humans, which, while potentially interesting, doesn't address the specific challenge of attributing immunological function across species. Eliminate Choice B because it merely restate information from the passage, focusing on gut bacteria research for humans rather than the challenge of determining immunological function across varied species. Eliminate Choice D because it makes a comparison, which is neither indicated nor implied in the text.

14. **Answer: A. Possessive punctuation.** Use the process of elimination looking for differences from the first word, then move to the right. Eliminate the first outlier Choice C, which uses the plural form *algorithms.* We need a possessive here. Next, eliminate Choice B because it uses a singular possessive form. Notice that right before the introductory information *deep learning,* there is no article (*a, an,* or *the*). This means that the word the possessive, **algorithms,** must be plural. (For instance, you would not say **Deep learning algorithm is good.** You would say *A deep learning algorithm is good.* Eliminate B since it uses a singular possessive. Now compare between A and D to notice that there is an apostrophe s on Choice D. Eliminate Choice D since the word **networks** is a noun.

15. **Answer: B. Punctuation.** Use process of elimination by moving from the first word to the right. Notice that there is a comma after the word **sculptor** on Choice A and Choice C. When you see a name, look at the beginning of the details associated with the name. Since there is no article (a, an or the), it means that you must remove the comma between the name and the information. Eliminate Choice A and C. Now, notice the comma at the end of **Tanaka.** Since **Tanaka** must connect to *constructed his robotic sculptures...* and since there is a comma before the predicate verb *constructed,* you need a comma after **Tanaka** to separate the interrupter *along with his team of tech-savvy artisans.* The corrected sentence here would be *eco-futurist and sculptor Akira Tanaka, along with his team of tech-savvy artisans, constructed his robotic sculptures...*

16. **Answer: D. IDP.** Break up each answer choice and identify the components from the first word to the first word that repeats in the answer choice, *programming.* Then identify the construction for each answer choice.

A) [INDEPENDENT] The Global Hour of Code, initiated by the international computer science education organization Code.org in 2013, is an event inspiring people worldwide to learn basic programming [DEPENDENT] and individuals interested in taking part can access tutorials and learning materials through the Code.org website or mobile application.

B) [INDEPENDENT] The Global Hour of Code, initiated by the international computer science education organization Code.org in 2013, is an event inspiring people worldwide to learn basic programming, [INDEPENDENT]individuals interested in taking part can access tutorials and learning materials through the Code.org website or mobile application.

C) [INDEPENDENT] The Global Hour of Code, initiated by the international computer science education organization Code.org in 2013, is an event inspiring people worldwide to learn basic programming [INDEPENDENT]individuals interested in taking part can access tutorials and learning materials through the Code.org website or mobile application.

D) [INDEPENDENT] The Global Hour of Code, initiated by the international computer science education organization Code.org in 2013, is an event inspiring people worldwide to learn basic programming; [INDEPENDENT]individuals interested in taking part can access tutorials and learning materials through the Code.org website or mobile application.

Now notice how each sentence is coded. Make sure to keep track of the punctuation.

A) I D = VALID
B) I, I = INVALID
C) I I = INVALID
D) I; I = VALID

Notice that A and D are valid constructions, but choice A begins a dependent clause with the word *and*. A dependent clause starting with the word AND requires a comma before it. Therefore, Choice D is the best answer.

17. **Answer: D. Misplaced modifier.** The word or phrase that follows the modifier *An iconic iron lattice structure in the city's skyline,* must be the object that this modifier describes. Choice A starts with **millions of visitors**; eliminate. Choice B starts with **attracting...**; eliminate. Choice C starts with **the Eiffel Tower's attractiveness**, not the Eiffel Tower. Choice D properly starts with the modified object.

18. **Answer: A. IDP.** Notice that the basic skeleton of the sentence is *Chen's study...will inform conservationists' efforts.* Choosing any other answer choice creates a giant fragment and an invalid construction.

19. **Answer: C. Subject-verb agreement.** Notice that A and B contain plural verbs, C contains a singular, and D is not a predicate verb. This means that you must connect the correct subject. To connect was/were/are to the word *doors* is what the question wants you to do. The word that actually connects to these verbs is *an exquisite chamber,* which then connects to *was* in Choice C.

20. **Answer: A. Punctuation.** Start with B because a colon requires an independent clause to the left of it. Notice that the colon placement after the construction *British naval officer Captain George S. Ritchie confirmed that the **Mariana Trench** ends abruptly.* **The Mariana Trench** needs a predicate

verb to complete the idea. Choice C connects **the Mariana Trench** with the predicate verb *exists*. However, it starts with a dash and closes with a comma; eliminate. Choice D is missing a comma. Choice A properly separates the interrupting information between **the Mariana Trench**…*exists*…

21. **Answer: A. Transitions.** To determine the most logical transition, let's analyze the relationship between the information before and after the blank. Before the blank, the text discusses the WHO's declaration that processed meats are carcinogenic, based on an IARC report classifying them as Group 1 carcinogens. After the blank, the text mentions that the report prompted a discussion about diet's role in cancer prevention and the importance of informed dietary choices. The information after the blank is a continuation and expansion of the implications of the report mentioned before the blank. Since the second sentence is describing an additional impact of the report, the additive transition in Choice A, **Moreover,** works best here. Eliminate Choice B because the lack of a contrast. Eliminate Choice C because **In other words** is used for clarification or emphasis, neither of which apply here. Eliminate Choice D because the following sentence is not an example of the previous sentence.

22. **Answer: A. Transitions.** Before the blank, the text discusses the Mars Curiosity rover's mission and its discovery of evidence suggesting Mars once had conditions that could have supported life. After the blank, the text mentions that the question of whether life existed on Mars is still unanswered, and scientists continue to analyze data to understand the planet's mysteries. The information after the blank presents a contrast or limitation to the implications of the discovery mentioned before. While the evidence suggests conditions that could have supported life, it doesn't definitively answer whether life actually existed. The contrasting transition **That being said**, used to introduce a contrast or a limitation of the previous statement, best fits here. Choice B's **That is** is a clarifying or an intensifying transition, restating a similar idea; eliminate. Choice C's **As a result** is a causal transition. The second sentence is not the result of the first; eliminate. Choice D **Elsewhere** suggests a shift to a different location or topic, which doesn't match the context of continuing the discussion about Mars.

23. **Answer: C. Transitions.** Before the blank, the text describes Alexander Fleming's observation of mold preventing bacterial growth in an experiment. After the blank, the text continues with Fleming's realization about the mold producing a substance that inhibits bacterial growth, leading to the discovery of penicillin. The information after the blank is a direct continuation and consequence of the observation mentioned before, so **subsequently,** used to introduce a following event, works best here. It connects the next step in Fleming's thought process and discovery. Eliminate Choice A; **however** is used to highlight a contrast. Eliminate Choice B; nevertheless is a concession or a limitation of the previous sentence. Eliminate Choice D; the second sentence is not a specific example of the generalization in the previous sentence.

24. **Answer: C. Transitions.** Before the blank, the text discusses the ancient Egyptians' architectural achievements, particularly their pyramids, and states that they are often credited with building the first pyramids. After the blank, the text provides specific information about the oldest known pyramid, the Pyramid of Djoser, including its construction date and dynasty. The information after the blank provides factual support and specificity to the general statement made before it. The transition

In fact, used to introduce a statement that confirms, emphasizes, or provides specific evidence for a previous, more general statement, works best here. Eliminate Choice A; **In addition** is used to add more information about the subject in the previous sentence. Eliminate Choice B; **Consequently** is used to describe the effect from the previous sentence. Eliminate Choice D; **Alternatively** is used to suggest a contrary perspective.

25. **Answer: D. Rhetorical synthesis.** Find the answer that support the question stem: **introduce the concept of cognitive restructuring to an audience already familiar with Cognitive Behavioral Therapy.** Choice A combines information about cognitive restructuring with details about CBT's development. While it mentions the key aspect of challenging and reframing thoughts, it includes the unnecessary phrase **developed by psychiatrist Aaron Beck**. This historical detail about CBT's origins is superfluous for an audience already familiar with CBT; eliminate. Choice B doesn't effectively introduce cognitive restructuring. It presents cognitive restructuring as an additional concept rather than focusing on explaining what it is, failing to provide a clear introduction to the technique; eliminate. Choice C is too general and doesn't specifically introduce cognitive restructuring. It broadly describes CBT's focus on thought patterns and behaviors without highlighting cognitive restructuring as a specific technique within CBT. Choice D focuses specifically on cognitive restructuring within the context of CBT. It succinctly explains what cognitive restructuring involves, **challenging and reframing distorted thoughts,** and connects it to the overall goal of improving mental health.

26. **Answer: C. Rhetorical synthesis.** Find the answer that supports the question stem: **emphasize a similarity in the anatomy between the two species.** Choice A focuses on the social structure differences between chimpanzees and bonobos. This information contrasts the two species rather than emphasizing an anatomical similarity; eliminate. Choice B merely states that chimpanzees and bonobos are the two extant species in the genus Pan. While this indicates a taxonomic relationship, it doesn't highlight any specific anatomical similarity; eliminate. Choice C focuses specifically on an anatomical similarity between chimpanzees and bonobos. It succinctly explains that **both species exhibit neocortical asymmetry, particularly in the planum temporale region**. This directly addresses the goal of emphasizing an anatomical similarity between the two species. Choice D mentions the evolutionary divergence of chimpanzees and bonobos from a common ancestor. While this implies similarities due to shared ancestry, it doesn't highlight a specific anatomical similarity; eliminate.

27. **Answer: D. Rhetorical synthesis.** Find the answer that supports the question stem: **introduce the adaptations and uses of bioluminescence to an audience already familiar with general concepts in marine biology.** Eliminate Choice A; it only produces information about bioluminescence itself. Eliminate Choice B; it only produces information about its uses. Eliminate Choice C; it only produces information about its adaptation. Choice D correctly identifies its adaptation (**evolved symbiotic bioluminescent bacteria in their gut**) and its uses (**produce light for camouflage, attraction of prey, and communication**).

TEST 2: MODULE 2 ANSWER EXPLANATIONS

1. **Answer: D. Vocab in context.** The excerpt describes Lady Emilia's internal struggle and the physical manifestations of her distress, suggesting that her face was involuntarily showing or displaying her emotional state.

2. **Answer: B. Sentence completion.** The clue is in the second clause after the semi-colon. It states that she was aware of the *apparent anomalies* (unusual aspects) in her data. This suggests that her initial hypothesis was considered weak or insufficient. The best word that fits this structure is **tenuous**, which means weak and insubstantial. **Disingenuous** in Choice A means dishonest; eliminate. **Revolutionary** in Choice C means momentous and significant; eliminate. **Indubitable** in Choice D means undoubtedly or absolute; eliminate.

3. **Answer: B. Sentence completion.** The clue is *Confirming what researchers have long suspected.* The study would then **corroborate** *the long-held belief.* **Undermine** in Choice A means weaken; eliminate. **Implement** in choice C means to put into action; eliminate. **Retract** in Choice D means to take back; eliminate.

4. **Answer: A. Sentence completion.** The clue is in the clause after the semi-colon. The phrase *were reshaping industries across the board* suggests that *the factors* were CAUSING *a significant shift.* The word that comes closest to causing is **precipitating**. **Obstructing** in choice B means blocking; eliminate. **Capitulating** in Choice D means surrendering; eliminate.

5. **Answer: C. Global.** Use process of elimination. Eliminate Choice A; it introduces Kovac's findings, but Haddad points out a problem with her study rather than presenting a theory of his own. Eliminate Choice B; the focus of the study is not explanatory. Eliminate Choice D; there is no comparison between the two types. Choice C correctly identifies **a potential limitation in the methodology** (*studying drug effects solely in cell cultures may oversimplify complex brain processes*) **of a neuroscience study** (*Dr. Elena Kovacs and colleagues published a study…*).

6. **Answer: B. Function.** Use process of elimination. Eliminate Choice A; it accurately summarizes the entire passage, but does not describe the function of the underlined excerpt. Eliminate Choice C; the phrase *over 10,000* suggests a large number, not a small one. Eliminate D; it's completely off topic. Choice B corresponds with the text; *over 10,000 disciples* = **extensive influence** and *throughout its 1,500-year history* = **legacy of Shaolin Kung Fun in martial arts history.**

7. **Answer: D. Global.** Notice that each answer has three parts. Evaluate the accuracy based on the first part of each answer, then repeat to the second, and then the third. Notice how each part is identified and eliminate any answer choice that contains an inaccuracy.

    A) It defines a psychological concept [ACCURATE], provides an example of how it manifests in behavior [ACCURATE], and then presents recent research that challenges the universality of the concept [INACCURATE] – it doesn't challenge the universality but confirms it through the fmri.

B) It introduces a psychological theory [ACCURATE], explains how individuals typically respond to it [ACCURATE], and then describes neurological evidence supporting the theory's existence [INACCURATE] – it confirms the universal aspect, not its existence.
C) It outlines a cognitive technique [INACCURATE] – it is a cognitive process, not a technique, discusses its practical implications in daily life [ACCURATE], and then explores how different academic disciplines approach its study [ACCURATE].
D) It presents a psychological phenomenon [ACCURATE], illustrates its application in a specific context [ACCURATE], and then describes new findings that expand our understanding of its nature and mechanisms [ACCURATE].

8. **Answer: C. Cross-text.** Text 1 introduces the problem. Text 2 provides Tanaka's solution: *RNAi-mediated lignin reduction could be a promising strategy for controlling invasive aquatic plants in freshwater ecosystems.* Eliminate Choice A; no one's looking to increase **the growth of invasive species.** Eliminate Choice B; Tanaka's solution is to *limit* not **enhance the expression of genes...** Eliminate Choice D; this is not mentioned anywhere.

9. **Answer: C. Detail.** Use process of elimination. Choice A is incorrect because while the text indicates that Dr. Stavrou's findings contradict some ancient accounts, it doesn't suggest that the knowledge of ancient Greek authors as inferior to archaeological findings, but rather that they recognize the limitations and biases in these literary sources. Choice B is incorrect because the passage explicitly mentions archaeological evidence like pottery fragments, coins, and shipwrecks as the basis for Dr. Stavrou's findings, rather than any new written records from the western Mediterranean that contradict Herodotus and Thucydides. Choice D is incorrect because the text doesn't discuss or compare the methods of dating artifacts used by Dr. Stavrou's team and classical historians, instead focusing on the types of evidence they rely on for their historical interpretations. Choice C is correct because the passage clearly contrasts Dr. Stavrou and her colleagues' use of material culture (*Greek pottery fragments, coins, and shipwrecks*) with classical historians' reliance on literary sources, directly supporting the statement that they likely utilize material culture rather than the literary sources typically used by classical historians (*traditional scholarship, based largely on literary sources like Herodotus and Thucydides*).

10. **Answer: D. Weakening claims.** First identify the claim: *that dark matter must be composed of extremely massive particles that interact weakly with ordinary matter, explaining why it's difficult to detect directly.* Choice A is incorrect because the misalignment between dark matter and visible matter distributions actually supports the idea that dark matter interacts weakly with ordinary matter, which aligns with the student's claim rather than weakening it. Choice B is incorrect because the greater abundance of dark matter compared to ordinary matter doesn't directly address the student's claim about the nature of dark matter particles or their interactions. Choice C is incorrect because unexpected concentrations of visible matter in regions with strong gravitational lensing don't necessarily contradict the student's claim about dark matter's properties, as this observation doesn't directly relate to dark matter particle characteristics. Choice D is correct because if dark matter particles are found to be much less massive than suggested by gravitational lensing analysis, it directly contradicts the student's claim that dark matter must be composed of "extremely massive particles," thus significantly weakening their argument about the nature of dark matter.

11. **Answer: C. Supporting the claim.** First identify the claim: whose syncretic approach in the 1960s fused Eastern calligraphic traditions with Western abstraction, engendering a novel basis for a cross-cultural dialogue within non-representational art. Choice A is incorrect because it claims that the fusion is incomplete (**not fully realizing, a true East-West synthesis**). Choice B is incorrect because although it discusses *a novel* basis=**transcending conventional,** it lacks the connection between East and the West Choice D is incorrect because it suggests that the work shows more Western attributes than Eastern ones. Choice C **seamless blend** = *fused Eastern…Western,* **unique cross-cultural** = *novel basis for a cross-cultural.*

12. **Answer: B. Infographics.** Use process of elimination. Choice A is incorrect because Academic support was indeed ranked lower for students (16) than it was for administration (3). While this statement is accurate based on the data, it is irrelevant to the researchers' conclusion about social skills being an important benefit for both teachers and students. Choice C is incorrect because while Stress reduction was ranked higher for students (7) than it was for teachers (4), this statement is accurate but irrelevant to the conclusion about the importance of social skills improvement. Choice D is incorrect because although Social skills was ranked higher for teachers (3) than it was for students (6), which is accurate, this statement is only partially relevant. It doesn't fully capture the researchers' conclusion that both groups viewed social skills improvement as important. The conclusion emphasizes the shared view of importance, not just the difference in rankings. Choice B is correct because it most closely aligns with the researchers' conclusion. Social skills was ranked very highly by teachers (3rd out of 20) and relatively highly by students (6th out of 20). This statement is both accurate and highly relevant, supporting the conclusion that both groups regard social skills improvement as an important benefit of after-school programs.

13. **Answer: B. Logical completions.** Follow the line of reasoning in the text: 1) MPAs are important for conserving ocean ecosystems and biodiversity. 2) MPAs face limitations from factors like illegal fishing, pollution, and climate change. 3) A more significant limitation is that many MPAs are small and isolated from each other. 4) This isolation hinders marine species' movement between protected areas and genetic diversity maintenance. The blank requires a link between the main limitation (isolated MPAs hindering species movement and genetic diversity) and a solution that specifically addresses this gap (interconnected MPA networks). Choice A is incorrect because focusing solely on establishing MPAs in areas with the highest biodiversity fails to address the connectivity issue. While it might protect species-rich areas, it could exacerbate the problem of isolation if these highly diverse areas are far apart. Choice C is incorrect because although mitigating climate change impacts is important, it doesn't directly solve the isolation problem of MPAs. Focusing on climate change without addressing connectivity could result in better-protected but still isolated areas. Choice D is incorrect because improved enforcement might better protect species within individual MPAs but wouldn't facilitate their movement between protected areas. This could lead to well-protected but genetically isolated populations, potentially reducing their long-term viability and adaptability. Choice B is correct because it directly addresses the main limitation discussed in the text. By prioritizing the creation of MPA networks that enhance connectivity between protected areas, this solution directly tackles the problem of isolation mentioned in points 3 and 4. It logically follows that improving connectivity would help marine species move between protected areas and maintain genetic diversity.

14. **Answer: B. Infographic & Supporting claims.** The claim to support from the graph is as follows: The [TECHNOLOGY] sector's contribution to Colorado's economy in 2023 stands out particularly in terms of its efficiency, outpacing many other industries in the state by maximizing revenue output through its revenue per employee. Choice A is incorrect because while it accurately states that the Technology sector generates the highest revenue in the state, it makes an unfounded claim about having the **smartest employees.** Choice C is incorrect because while it correctly identifies that the Technology sector achieves the highest revenue, it inaccurately claims that Technology (180,000) has the fewest employees; Manufacturing does (125,000). Choice D is incorrect because it only partially represents the data accurately. While it correctly states that the Technology sector produces the highest revenue, it incorrectly claims it has the greatest number of employees.

15. **Answer: D. Logical completion.** Follow the line of reasoning. 1) Spiral galaxies were less common, and elliptical galaxies more common, in the early universe compared to the local (present-day) universe. 2) Galaxies in the early universe were generally smaller with higher star formation rates relative to their mass compared to local galaxies. 3) In the local universe, larger galaxies typically have lower star formation rates relative to their mass (known as "galaxy quenching"). This trend was less pronounced in the early universe. 4) Locally, elliptical galaxies are typically larger with lower star formation rates than spiral galaxies. Choice A is incorrect because it is contradicted earlier in the passage *galaxies in the early universe were generally smaller and had <u>higher star formation rates</u> relative to their mass compared to galaxies in the local universe.* Choice B is incorrect because it introduces a new concept about the rate of galactic collisions remaining constant throughout the universe's history. Choice C is incorrect because it contradicts the finding that early galaxies generally had higher star formation rates relative to their mass compared to local galaxies. There's no info suggesting early spirals deviated from this general trend. Choice D logically follows from the findings. The trend of lower star formation rates relative to mass in larger, local galaxies (quenching), combined with the observation that this trend was less pronounced in the early universe, supports the conclusion that star formation rate is negatively correlated with cosmic time—older galaxies generally forming fewer stars relative to their mass than younger ones.

16. **Answer: A. Punctuation & IDP.** Identify the components of the excerpt.

    A) [INDEPENDENT] During the rapid evolution of robotics in the 20th century, several breakthroughs were crucial: [PHRASE] the invention of the first digitally operated robot, Unimate, in 1961, for instance. [INDEPENDENT] The development of WABOT-1, a first full-scale humanoid intelligent robot, in 1973 is another such milestone.

    B) [INDEPENDENT] During the rapid evolution of robotics in the 20th century, several breakthroughs were crucial: [PHRASE] the invention of the first digitally operated robot, Unimate, in 1961, for instance, [INDEPENDENT] the development of WABOT-1, a first full-scale humanoid intelligent robot, in 1973 is another such milestone.

    C) [INDEPENDENT] During the rapid evolution of robotics in the 20th century, several breakthroughs were crucial: [PHRASE] the invention of the first digitally operated robot, Unimate, in 1961. [INDEPENDENT] for instance, the development of WABOT-1, a first full-scale humanoid intelligent robot, in 1973 is another such milestone.

D) [INDEPENDENT] During the rapid evolution of robotics in the 20th century, several breakthroughs were crucial: [PHRASE] the invention of the first digitally operated robot, Unimate, in 1961 for instance, [INDEPENDENT] The development of WABOT-1, a first full-scale humanoid intelligent robot, in 1973 is another such milestone.

Now examine the configurations:

A) I: P. I = VALID
B) I: P, I = INVALID
C) I: P. I = VALID
D) I: P, I = INVALID

First eliminate B and D. Although P, I is an acceptable configuration following a colon, the positioning of the phrase turns it into a modifier for the subject noun *WABOT*-1 in the second clause. These two constructions create a comma splice. Now, examine the difference between A and B. To figure out where the *for instance* should be placed, notice that the sentence is identifying two breakthroughs: the first robot, *Unimate* and the second robot, *WABOT-1*. Now, notice that the **for instance** is used to describe *Unimate*. *WABOT-1 ... is another.* This means that the for instance should be included within the description of *Unimate*. Here is a visual breakdown of the two sentences.

1) During the rapid evolution of robotics in the 20th century, several breakthroughs were crucial: the invention of the first digitally operated robot, Unimate, in 1961, for instance.

The development of WABOT-1, a first full-scale humanoid intelligent robot, in 1973 is another such milestone.

17. **Answer: A. Misplaced modifier.** Notice that the sentence begins with the modifier *Knowing these silicone-based lifeforms...* The word that immediately follows the comma should be the object or person who know these silicone-based forms. Choice A starts with **the researchers**; keep. Choice B starts with **wormholes**; eliminate. Choice C starts with **reorientation**; eliminate. Choice D starts with **the researchers' theory**, not the researchers; eliminate.

18. **Answer: D. IDP.** This looks like a subject verb question where you would have to line up *member* with either **agreed** or **agrees.** However, this is actually testing your understanding of clauses and punctuation. Notice that the first part of this sentence is an independent clause.

    Mexico, Canada, and the United States, signatories of the United States-Mexico-Canada Agreement, or USMCA, have jointly embraced the principles of free trade in North America,

    This means that the second part of this sentence must be a phrase or a dependent clause. Choosing A, B, or C creates a comma splice, which is invalid. Choice D creates a phrase *each member* **agreeing...**

19. **Answer: A. Punctuation.** Here, you need to determine whether the two countries, *Luxembourg and Greece,* are essential or non-essential elements. The word *respective* means that they are essential, otherwise the sentence wouldn't make sense. Choice A allows you to link the percentages to the

countries. In contrast, eliminate B, since it removes the necessary components. Here's an example of what Choice B is essentially saying:

> B) For instance, in 2021, the United States spent 3.57% of its GDP on defense, while fellow NATO nations spent 0.58% and 3.82% of their respective GDPs on defense.

Notice that the word *respective* requires that there be two countries to line up with the 0.58% and 3.82%. By using commas around B, the countries become non-essential and the idea behind the sentence remains incomplete.

Next, eliminate Choice C because the comma turns the subject into an interrupter, disconnects the predicate verb *spent* from the **nations Luxembourg and Greece** and connects it to the United States. This is what Choice C is essentially saying.

> C) For instance, in 2021, the United States spent 3.57% of its GDP on defense spent 0.58% and 3.82% of their respective GDPs on defense.

Finally, eliminate Choice D as it creates an unnecessary list of three objects: *fellow NATO nations,* **Luxembourg, and Greece**.

20. **Answer: D. IDP.** Break up the components of the sentence.

A) [INDEPENDENT] Like many of the Mariana Trench's inhabitants, the snailfish, which resides at depths of up to 8,200 meters, is adapted to extreme conditions, [PHRASE] while sporting a translucent, scaleless body, [INDEPENDENT] the pinkish-white fish withstands pressures up to 1,000 times that of sea level.

B) [INDEPENDENT] Like many of the Mariana Trench's inhabitants, the snailfish, which resides at depths of up to 8,200 meters, is adapted to extreme conditions [PHRASE] while sporting a translucent, scaleless body, [INDEPENDENT] the pinkish-white fish withstands pressures up to 1,000 times that of sea level.

C) [INDEPENDENT] Like many of the Mariana Trench's inhabitants, the snailfish, which resides at depths of up to 8,200 meters, is adapted to extreme conditions, [PHRASE] sporting a translucent, scaleless body, [INDEPENDENT] the pinkish-white fish withstands pressures up to 1,000 times that of sea level.

D) [INDEPENDENT] Like many of the Mariana Trench's inhabitants, the snailfish, which resides at depths of up to 8,200 meters, is adapted to extreme conditions: [PHRASE] sporting a translucent, scaleless body, [INDEPENDENT] the pinkish-white fish withstands pressures up to 1,000 times that of sea level.

Now examine the configurations and notice that A, B, and C are all comma splices while D is the only valid configuration:

A) I, P, I = INVALID
B) I, P, I = INVALID
C) I, P, I = INVALID

D) I: P, I = VALID

21. **Answer: B. Transitions.** To determine the most logical transition, let's analyze the relationship between the sentences and the information they convey: The first sentence introduces the ASA A14 standards from 1932. The second sentence mentions that ASA A14 replaced the 1923 National Safety Council guidelines. The third sentence (which needs the transition) provides information about the 1923 guidelines, specifically that they sparked a debate and were not mandatory. Let's consider each option:

    A) **For instance,** - This would be used to give an example.
    B) **Nevertheless,** - This indicates a contrast or contradiction to the previous information.
    C) **Moreover,** - This is used to add information that supports or extends the previous point.
    D) **Likewise,** - This suggests a similarity or comparison.

    The most logical transition here is **Nevertheless,** The passage mentions that the 1923 guidelines were replaced. The next sentence clarifies that it still had an important impact. The word **Nevertheless** effectively introduces this contrasting information about the nature of the earlier guidelines.

22. **Answer: A. Transitions.** Let's analyze the relationship between the sentences to determine the most logical transition: The first sentence states that many iconic landmarks were built quickly, in just a few years. The second sentence (needing the transition) introduces a contrasting idea: not all famous structures were built quickly. The third sentence provides an example of a structure that took a very long time to build. Now, let's consider each option:

    A) **Granted,** - This is used to acknowledge a point that contrasts with the main argument.
    B) **Fittingly,** - This suggests that what follows is appropriate or suitable.
    C) **That is,** - This is used to clarify or restate something.
    D) **Ultimately,** - This typically introduces a final point or conclusion.

    Granted, effectively bridges the gap between the quick construction of some landmarks and the introduction of examples that took much longer. It acknowledges the truth of the first statement while preparing the reader for contrasting information.

23. **Answer: A. Transitions.** Let's analyze the relationship between the sentences to determine the most logical transition: The first sentence introduces a study that determined the ratio of three plant subtypes in moose diets. The second sentence (needing the transition) expands on what the researchers did beyond just classifying plant types--they *measured the comparative volumes*. Now, let's consider each option:

    A) **Notably,** - This is used to draw attention to an important or significant point.
    B) **Instead,** - This suggests a replacement or alternative.
    C) **Later,** - This indicates a chronological sequence.
    D) **For example,** - This is used to introduce a specific instance of a preceding generalization.

    Notably, works well because the intensifying transition emphasizes that the researchers didn't just stop at identifying plant types, but went further to determine relative quantities. This additional step is a significant aspect of the study that deserves attention.

24. **Answer: B. Transitions.** Let's analyze the relationship between the sentences to determine the most logical transition: The first sentence discusses the Treaty of Versailles, its significance in ending World War I, and its impact on Western Europe, particularly Germany. The second sentence (needing the transition) shifts focus to another significant consequence of World War I: changes in the former Ottoman Empire. Now, let's consider each option:

    A) **Regardless,** - This suggests a contrast or lack of relevance, which doesn't fit here.
    B) **Elsewhere,** - This indicates a shift in geographical focus, which could be appropriate.
    C) **In fact,** - This is used to emphasize or add stronger information to a previous point.
    D) **Specifically,** - This is used to provide more detailed information about a previously mentioned topic.

    Elsewhere, works well because it maintains the theme of post-WWI changes while clearly indicating a shift in geographical focus from Western Europe to the former Ottoman Empire. It helps the reader understand that the passage is now discussing parallel but geographically distinct consequences of the war's end.

25. **Answer: A. Rhetorical synthesis.** Find the answers that support the question stem: **emphasize the size of pit.** Eliminate Choice B; it references the size of the particle, not the pit. Eliminate Choice D; it focuses on the formation rather than the size of the pit. Notice that Choice A and C both reference the size, but Choice A uses *incredibly tiny* to emphasize its size.

26. **Answer: D. Rhetorical synthesis.** Find the answer that supports the question stem: **make and support a generalization about bioluminescence.** Eliminate A; it contains two generalizations. Eliminate Choice B; it only provides an example. Eliminate Choice C; it contains two generalizations. Choice D correctly makes a generalization (**Marine…purposes**) and supports the generalization (**the firefly…communicate**).

27. **Answer: D. Rhetorical synthesis.** Find the answer that supports the question stem: **a specific example of a poetic form.** Eliminate Choice A; it discusses a poetic technique, not form. Eliminate Choice B; it makes the same error as A. Eliminate Choice C; it provides a general definition of poetry. Choice D describes haiku, which is a specific poetic form. It accurately uses information from the notes, mentioning that haiku has "three unrhymed lines containing five, seven, and five syllables respectively." This directly relates to the definition provided in the notes.

Reading and Writing

32 MINUTES, 27 QUESTIONS

DIRECTIONS

The questions in this section address a number of important reading and writing skills. Each question includes one or more passages, which may include a table or graph. Read each passage and question carefully, and then choose the best answer to the question based on the passage(s).

All questions in this section are multiple-choice with four answer choices. Each question has a single best answer.

1

The soft whispers of the wind <u>wove</u> through the rustling leaves, creating a gentle symphony in the tranquil forest. Birds chirped their melodies, harmonizing with the soothing sounds of a nearby stream, their notes complementing the natural ambiance.

As used in the text, what does the word "wove" most nearly mean?

A) formed
B) mingled
C) escaped
D) interlocked

2

The new regulations imposed by the government have made it _____ for small businesses to operate profitably, leading many to shut down or significantly reduce their workforce.

Which choice completes the text with the most logical and precise word or phrase?

A) imperative
B) misconstrued
C) prohibitive
D) conducive

Edenbrook Test 3

3

The highly anticipated debate between the two rival politicians with a history of disdain for each other was about to begin, and the atmosphere in the auditorium was electric. The tension in the room was _____ as the candidates took the stage, with supporters from both sides eagerly awaiting the first verbal jabs.

Which choice completes the text with the most logical and precise word or phrase?

A) imperceptible
B) insignificant
C) palpable
D) pretentious

4

The young entrepreneur's business plan was thorough and well-researched, with every detail meticulously outlined and supported by relevant data. However, the inclusion of a 50-page appendix containing _____ information that had little bearing on the core proposal ultimately detracted from the overall effectiveness of the presentation.

Which choice completes the text with the most logical and precise word or phrase?

A) superfluous
B) paramount
C) pertinent
D) succinct

5

The author's latest novel, a gripping tale of love, loss, and redemption in a war-torn nation, was met with widespread praise from critics and readers alike. The book's vivid characters, intricate plot, and thought-provoking themes earned her _____ from even the most discerning literary circles, further solidifying her position as one of the most influential writers of her generation.

Which choice completes the text with the most logical and precise word or phrase?

A) acclaim
B) repudiation
C) ambivalence
D) prevalence

6

"The discovery of microscopic fossils in ancient rock formations has revolutionized our understanding of early life on Earth," explains Dr. Elena Rodriguez, a paleobiologist at the University of Cambridge. "These tiny remnants provide a window into ecosystems that existed billions of years ago, long before complex life forms emerged. By studying these microfossils, we can piece together the story of how life evolved and adapted to Earth's changing conditions over vast stretches of time."

Which choice best states the main purpose of the text?

A) To highlight the technological advancements that have made microfossil discovery possible
B) To compare the study of microfossils to other methods of investigating early Earth history
C) To emphasize the significance of microfossils in reconstructing a narrative
D) To argue for increased funding and resources to be allocated to microfossil research

7

The following text is from Paul Laurence Dunbar's 1913 poem *The Paradox*.

> I am the mother of sorrows,
> I am the ender of grief;
> I am the bud and the blossom,
> I am the late-falling leaf.
> I am thy priest and thy poet,
> I am thy serf and thy king;
> I cure the tears of the heartsick,
> When I come near they shall sing.
> White are my hands as the snowdrop;
> Swart are my fingers as clay;
> Dark is my frown as the midnight,
> Fair is my brow as the day.

Which choice best states the main purpose of the text?

A) To emphasize the speaker's role as a healer and comforter to those who suffer

B) To describe the speaker's physical appearance and its contrasting elements

C) To suggest the speaker's struggle with their own sense of self and purpose

D) To highlight the contradictory and multifaceted nature of the speaker's identity

8

The following text is from a poem titled *The Dancer*

> Lithe limbs in motion, a figure takes the stage,
> Expressing passion, joy, and tender rage.
> Each step a story, each gesture a phrase,
> The dancer's art, a fleeting moment ablaze.
> In the spotlight's glow, a world comes alive,
> A wordless tale, through movement to survive.
> <u>The music swells, the dancer's form takes flight,</u>
> <u>Defying gravity, embracing the night.</u>

Which choice best describes the function of the underlined sentence in the text as a whole?

A) It emphasizes the technical difficulty of the dancer's movements.

B) It highlights the ephemeral nature of the dancer's performance.

C) It suggests the dancer's struggle against physical limitations.

D) It underscores the skill and artistry characteristic of the dancer's abilities.

9

The following text is adapted from Mark Twain's 1884 novel *Adventures of Huckleberry Finn*.

> The sun was up so high when I waked that I judged it was after eight o'clock. I laid there in the grass and the cool shade thinking about things, and feeling rested and ruther comfortable and satisfied. I could see the sun out at one or two holes, but mostly it was big trees all about, and gloomy in there amongst them. There was freckled places on the ground where the light sifted down through the leaves, and the freckled places swapped about a little, showing there was a little breeze up there.

Which choice best describes the overall structure of the text?

A) It establishes the setting and then describes the character's emotions in that setting.

B) It presents the character's actions and then explains the reasons behind those actions.

C) It reveals the character's reflections and then provides a more detailed observation of the surroundings.

D) It portrays the character's memories and then contrasts them with the character's current situation.

10

In his groundbreaking work, "On the Origin of Species," Charles Darwin proposed the theory of evolution by natural selection. Darwin's theory suggests that organisms with traits that are advantageous for survival and reproduction are more likely to pass on their genes to future generations. Over time, this process of differential survival and reproduction leads to changes in populations and, ultimately, to the formation of new species. Darwin's theory was based on his observations of the natural world, including his famous voyage on the HMS Beagle, during which he studied the diverse flora and fauna of various regions, particularly the Galápagos Islands.

According to the passage, what did Charles Darwin study during his voyage on the HMS Beagle?

A) The process by which organisms with beneficial reproduce more successfully, leading to gradual changes in populations over time

B) The variety of plant and animal life in different areas of the Galápagos Islands

C) The importance of flora over fauna in various regions of the Galápagos Islands

D) The mating habits of various bird species on the Galápagos Islands

11

In his book *The Structure of Scientific Revolutions*, Thomas Kuhn argues that scientific progress is not a linear accumulation of knowledge but rather occurs through periodic paradigm shifts. He describes how scientists operate within a prevailing paradigm until anomalies arise that cannot be explained by the current framework, writing, _____

Which quotation from *The Structure of Scientific Revolutions* most effectively illustrates the claim?

A) "Normal science, the activity in which most scientists inevitably spend almost all their time, is predicated on the assumption that the scientific community knows what the world is like."

B) "The genesis of scientific discovery often lies in the persistent recognition of empirical incongruities that compel investigators to reexamine the foundational premises of their established frames of reference."

C) "The decision to reject one paradigm is always simultaneously the decision to accept another, and the judgment leading to that decision involves the comparison of both paradigms with nature and with each other."

D) "Almost always the men who achieve these fundamental inventions of a new paradigm have been either very young or very new to the field whose paradigm they change."

12

Researchers studying the impact of invasive species on native ecosystems found that the presence of invasive zebra mussels in North American lakes led to clearer water. They hypothesized that the mussels, known for their filtration abilities, were removing large amounts of phytoplankton and other suspended particles from the water column, thus increasing water clarity. However, the researchers also noted that the increased water clarity allowed more sunlight to penetrate deeper into the lakes, potentially causing a proliferation of aquatic plants and algae.

Which finding, if true, would most directly undermine the researchers' hypothesis?

A) In a controlled experiment, researchers found that the removal of phytoplankton and suspended particles by zebra mussels led to a decrease in the growth rates of aquatic plants and algae.

B) In some lakes with invasive zebra mussels, the population of native mussels has decreased significantly since the introduction of the invasive species.

C) In a controlled experiment, researchers found that the removal of phytoplankton and suspended particles by zebra mussels led to a decrease in the growth rates of aquatic plants and algae, as these organisms compete for the same nutrient resources.

D) In several lakes with established zebra mussel populations, water clarity has decreased compared to the period before the mussels were introduced.

13

Previous research has shown that insect species with a narrow geographical range tend to be more genetically homogeneous than insect species with extensive ranges are. Based on these findings, researchers recently ran simulations to predict how the genetic variation of several species of *Apidae*, a family of bees found throughout the world, might change in different distribution conditions. One of these species, *Bombus affinis*, is found only in the northeastern United States. The researchers simulated what would happen if *B. affinis* spread to new habitats outside the northeastern states, and, consistent with previous findings, the results showed that _____.

Which choice most logically completes the text?

A) the genetic homogeneity of *Apidae* species decreased in states neighboring the northeastern states.

B) the genetic homogeneity of *B. affinis* increased as it spread to habitats outside the northeastern states.

C) the genetic diversity of *B. affinis* decreased in states neighboring the northeastern states.

D) the genetic diversity of *B. affinis* increased as it spread to habitats outside the northeastern states.

14

Mentions of Selected Foods in English Literature and Popularity, 1300-1900

Food Item	First Known Mention	Number of Mentions Recorded	Popularity Index
Apple Pie	1390	112	8
Roast Beef	1315	534	37
Bread Pudding	1596	76	5
Tea	1657	2036	92

Researchers analyzed mentions of selected foods in English literature from 1300 to 1900 to understand the popularity and significance of these foods over time. They recorded the first known mention, the total number of mentions, and a popularity index for each food item. The popularity index was calculated based on factors such as the frequency of mentions, the context in which the foods were mentioned, and their cultural significance. The researchers concluded that the frequency of mentions and the popularity index in literature reflect the cultural importance and popularity of these foods in English society during the studied period.

Which choice best describes data from the graph that support the researchers' conclusion?

A) Roast beef had the second-highest popularity index at 37, behind only tea at 92. However, roast beef was mentioned 1315 times, the third-highest total mentions, while apple pie was mentioned only 112 times despite having the second-highest popularity index of 8.

B) Tea was mentioned far more than any other food item with the highest popularity index. In contrast, apple pie, the food with the latest first known mention in 1657, only had 112 total mentions despite its long history.

C) Tea had 2036 mentions and the highest popularity index of 92, while bread pudding had only 76 mentions and the lowest popularity index of 5.

D) First mentioned in 1596, Bread pudding had the lowest popularity index at 5, while first mentioned in 1390, Apple pie had the third lowest popularity index at 8, suggesting that neither were very popular.

Edenbrook Test 3

15

South Korea is widely recognized as one of the two most technologically advanced nations in Asia, alongside Japan. Although the country's status as a tech powerhouse is well-established, many still question the story behind how _____

Which choice completes the text so that it conforms to the conventions of Standard English?

A) was that power achieved?

B) was that power achieved.

C) that power was achieved?

D) that power was achieved.

16

In exchange for modest fees, 3D printer companies provide would-be entrepreneurs with the equipment, training, and customer base they need to succeed. _____ would be wise to consider working with 3D printer companies.

Which choice completes the text so that it conforms to the conventions of Standard English?

A) Anyone, interested in starting a 3D printing business,

B) Anyone interested, in starting a 3D printing business,

C) Anyone interested in starting a 3D printing business

D) Anyone interested in starting, a 3D printing business

17

The appearance of Halley's Comet in 1066 is one of the most well-documented astronomical events in history, as it was famously depicted in the Bayeux Tapestry. A recent study of tree ring figures from Eastern and Central Europe by researchers Maria Kovacs and Luka Novak _____ a compelling case that subtle yet significant changes in weather patterns played an essential role in this historic celestial occurrence.

Which choice completes the text so that it conforms to the conventions of Standard English?

A) have presented

B) presenting

C) present

D) presents

18

K-pop has taken the world by storm with its catchy tunes and mesmerizing performances. As they dance their way, like synchronized machines, against a dazzling backdrop of stage _____ seem designed to be photographed.

Which choice completes the text so that it conforms to the conventions of Standard English?

A) lights; the K-pop idols

B) lights, the K-pop idols

C) lights, the K-pop idols,

D) lights the K-pop idols

19

To twenty-first-century scientists, the idea of manipulating genes seemed like the perfect response to the rapid increase in genetic disorders and agricultural challenges. Thus, _____ was hailed as a precise and efficient way to correct disease-causing mutations, enhance crop yields, and improve livestock while meeting the growing demand for healthier and more sustainable food production.

Which choice completes the text so that it conforms to the conventions of Standard English?

A) CRISPR or Clustered Regularly Interspaced Short Palindromic Repeats

B) CRISPR, or Clustered Regularly Interspaced Short Palindromic Repeats,

C) CRISPR--or Clustered Regularly Interspaced Short Palindromic Repeats,

D) CRISPR, or Clustered Regularly Interspaced Short Palindromic Repeats

20

At Johnson & Johnson, Smith and his team collaborate with external partners—pharmaceutical research institutes—to develop new medications for diseases under investigation. The research institutes' scientists, many of whom have earned a doctoral degree in pharmacology or a related _____ use cutting-edge laboratory equipment such as high-performance liquid chromatography systems that isolate and characterize drug compounds.

Which choice completes the text with the most logical transition?

A) field and
B) field. They
C) field,
D) field; moreover, they

21

The blue whale is the largest animal known to have ever existed on Earth; _____ the largest blue whale ever recorded was a staggering 110 feet long and weighed an estimated 200 tons.

Which choice completes the text with the most logical transition?

A) furthermore,
B) in contrast,
C) in fact,
D) on the other hand,

22

The planet Venus is often referred to as Earth's "sister planet" due to their similar size and composition; _____ scientists have been interested in studying Venus to better understand the potential outcomes of runaway greenhouse effects and the evolution of planetary atmospheres.

Which choice completes the text with the most logical transition?

A) nevertheless,
B) accordingly,
C) for instance,
D) conversely,

Edenbrook Test 3

23

The Great Wall of China is often cited as the only man-made structure visible from space. This is a common misconception, _____ as the Great Wall is not visible from low Earth orbit, and even less so from the Moon.

Which choice completes the text with the most logical transition?

A) in addition,

B) in fact,

C) in other words,

D) however,

24

The team had practiced diligently for weeks, pouring their hearts into every training session; _____ they found themselves outmatched by their opponents during the championship game.

Which choice completes the text with the most logical transition?

A) in fact,

B) specifically,

C) for all that,

D) additionally,

25

While researching a topic, a student has taken the following notes:

- Phytoplankton are microscopic algae that form the base of the marine food chain, with most species ranging from 2 to 200 micrometers in size.
- Copepods are small crustaceans that feed on phytoplankton and range in size from 0.5 to 2 millimeters, with the largest species growing up to 32 centimeters.
- Phytoplankton are responsible for producing about 50% of the Earth's oxygen through photosynthesis.
- Copepods are a crucial link in the marine food chain, transferring energy from phytoplankton to larger animals like fish and whales.
- Despite their small size, phytoplankton can form massive blooms that can be seen from space, covering hundreds of square kilometers.
- Copepods are also important prey for many fish species, and their abundance can influence the population dynamics of commercially important fish stocks.

The student wants to contrast the relative sizes of the two organisms. Which choice most effectively uses relevant information from the notes to accomplish this goal?

A) Phytoplankton form the base of the marine food chain, while copepods are small crustaceans that feed on phytoplankton and other microscopic organisms.

B) Phytoplankton range from 2 to 200 micrometers, while copepods are typically 0.5 to 2 millimeters in size, with some species reaching up to 32 centimeters

C) Phytoplankton produce about 50% of Earth's oxygen through photosynthesis, whereas copepods transfer energy from phytoplankton to larger marine animals.

D) Phytoplankton can form massive blooms visible from space, while copepods are crucial prey for many fish species, influencing commercial fish stocks.

26

While researching a topic, a student has taken the following notes:

- Electric cars produce zero direct emissions, reducing air pollution in urban areas.
- The batteries in electric cars can be recharged using renewable energy sources like solar and wind power.
- The production of electric car batteries requires mining rare earth metals, which can cause environmental damage.
- The electricity used to charge electric cars often comes from power plants that burn fossil fuels, indirectly contributing to greenhouse gas emissions.
- The disposal of electric car batteries at the end of their life can be challenging and may lead to environmental concerns if not handled properly.

The student wants to explain a disadvantage of electric cars. Which choice most effectively uses relevant information from the notes to accomplish this goal?

A) Electric cars can indirectly contribute to greenhouse gas emissions when the electricity used to charge them comes from power plants that burn fossil fuels.

B) The batteries in electric cars can be recharged using renewable energy sources, reducing the reliance on fossil fuels.

C) While electric cars can cause environmental damage and concerns, they produce zero direct emissions.

D) Electric cars help reduce air pollution in urban areas by producing zero direct emissions, but they may still indirectly contribute to pollution elsewhere.

27

While researching a topic, a student has taken the following notes:

- A study was conducted to investigate the effects of a new medication on patients with type 2 diabetes.
- The researchers recruited 500 participants diagnosed with type 2 diabetes and divided them into two groups: a treatment group receiving the new medication and a control group receiving a placebo.
- Participants were monitored for 12 weeks, with their blood glucose levels, insulin sensitivity, and body weight measured at regular intervals.
- The study found that participants in the treatment group experienced significant improvements in blood glucose control, insulin sensitivity, and body weight compared to the control group.
- The researchers caution that the study only included participants with type 2 diabetes, so the results may not be generalizable to patients with other types of diabetes or related conditions.

A student wants to summarize the results of the study. Which choice most effectively uses relevant information from the notes to accomplish this goal?

A) The treatment group experienced significant improvements in blood glucose control, insulin sensitivity, and body weight.

B) Researchers recruited 500 participants, divided into treatment and control groups, monitored for 12 weeks.

C) The study aimed to investigate the effects of a new medication on patients with type 2 diabetes, a condition characterized by high blood glucose levels and reduced insulin sensitivity.

D) Although the study found promising results for the new medication, researchers warn that the results may not be generalizable to patients with other types of diabetes or related conditions.

STOP

Reading and Writing

32 MINUTES, 27 QUESTIONS

DIRECTIONS

The questions in this section address a number of important reading and writing skills. Each question includes one or more passages, which may include a table or graph. Read each passage and question carefully, and then choose the best answer to the question based on the passage(s).

All questions in this section are multiple-choice with four answer choices. Each question has a single best answer.

1

The prototype seemed sufficiently capable of working in the field. However, after careful consideration, the company decided it would be most _____ to halt the project and cut their losses before investing any more resources.

Which choice completes the text with the most logical and precise word or phrase?

A) prudent
B) derelict
C) pernicious
D) indifferent

2

Much was riding on the politician's performance in the debate. Unfortunately, the politician's arguments were _____, lacking substance and designed merely to mislead the public.

Which choice completes the text with the most logical and precise word or phrase?

A) coherent
B) succinct
C) spurious
D) dilatory

3

The government flexed its military muscle by demonstrating its technology over a series of propagandic films. In an act of defiance, the rebels vowed to _____ the corrupt government and establish a new, just system in its place.

Which choice completes the text with the most logical and precise word or phrase?

A) delegate
B) topple
C) renounce
D) invalidate

4

The emperor deployed his army to the East to save its capital city. Instead, the conquering army decided to _____ the defeated city to the ground, leaving nothing but rubble and ashes in their wake.

Which choice completes the text with the most logical and precise word or phrase?

A) raze
B) remonstrate
C) recapitulate
D) reprove

5

Text 1
Archaeological studies rely heavily on reverse engineering, a controversial approach that infers past behaviors and technologies from artifacts. Proponents argue that analyzing the chaîne opératoire of objects can reconstruct ancient technical choices, social structures, and cultural norms. However, critics contend that this method is speculative and risks imposing modern biases, leading to ethnocentric interpretations.

Text 2
Archaeologists using reverse engineering engage in experimental archaeology, replicating ancient technologies with period-appropriate materials and techniques. These experiments provide insights into knowledge transmission, labor organization, and the role of material culture. Yet, the limitations of the archaeological record and the inability to fully recreate past contexts may lead to unwarranted speculation, necessitating a reflexive and multivocal approach to archaeological hermeneutics.

Based on the information in Text 2, how would the author most likely respond to the critics in Text 1?

A) The author would largely agree with the critics, suggesting that the speculative nature of reverse engineering severely limits its ability to fully recreate past contexts.

B) The author would suggest that the insights gained from experimental archaeology, as a key component of reverse engineering, are sufficient to counter the critics' concerns about speculation and ethnocentrism.

C) The author would argue that while the critics raise valid concerns, these can be mitigated by employing several techniques to archaeological interpretation.

D) The author would strongly disagree with the critics, maintaining that reverse engineering, when properly applied, is an empirically grounded method for understanding past technologies and behaviors.

Edenbrook Test 3

6

Did you know that Lewis Carroll's periodical *The Rectory Magazine* was written when he was only 13 years old? <u>Juvenilia, or works that an author produced as a youth before attaining fame, are becoming more and more popular among readers of all ages.</u> Some scholars think that this growth in popularity might be occurring because juvenilia could potentially reveal aspects of a writer's childhood.

Which choice best describes the function of the underlined portion in the text as a whole?

A) To introduce the topic of Lewis Carroll's *The Rectory Magazine* and its significance

B) To provide an example of a famous author's early work and its popularity

C) To suggest that Carroll's periodical was not well-received during his lifetime

D) To define the term "juvenilia" and assert its growing appeal

7

Scientists believed that periodical cicada emergence patterns were primarily influenced by environmental cues such as tree growth and weather conditions. However, a recent study has provided new insights into the factors influencing these patterns. By analyzing historical data and conducting field experiments, the researchers discovered that soil temperature plays a crucial role in triggering the cicadas' emergence. The study found that cicadas begin to emerge when soil temperatures reach approximately 64°F (18°C) at a depth of 8 inches. This finding suggests that climate change could potentially alter the timing of cicada emergences in the future, as global temperatures continue to rise.

Which choice best states the main idea of the text?

A) Cicadas emerge from the ground when soil temperatures reach a specific depth at a specific temperature.

B) Soil temperature, rather than previously assumed factors, is the primary trigger for periodical cicada emergence.

C) Climate change will cause cicadas to emerge earlier in the year, disrupting their natural cycles, when the temperature hits 64°F.

D) The findings from the new study on soil temperature could alter the the timing of cicada emergence.

8

The following text is adapted from a 19th century novel. Dorothea Brooke, a young woman, is reflecting on her life.

> Dorothea had gathered emotion as she went on, and had forgotten everything except the relief of pouring forth her feelings, unchecked: an experience once habitual with her, but hardly ever present since her marriage, which had been a perpetual struggle of energy with fear. For the moment, Will's admiration was accompanied with a chilling sense of remoteness. A man is seldom ashamed of feeling that he cannot love a woman so well when he sees a certain greatness in her: nature having intended greatness for men. But nature has sometimes made sad oversights in carrying out her intention; as in the case of good Mr. Brooke, whose masculine consciousness was at this moment in rather a stammering condition under the eloquence of his niece.

Which choice best describes what is happening in the text?

A) Dorothea is expressing herself with uncharacteristic emotional openness, prompting a reassessment of perceptions.

B) Dorothea is arguing with Will about the nature of love and greatness, leaving Mr. Brooke confused.

C) Will is professing his love for Dorothea, causing her to feel emotional and Mr. Brooke to feel uncomfortable.

D) Mr. Brooke is attempting to express his feelings to Dorothea, but her emotional response leaves him uncertain.

9

Researchers have been studying the impact of the European green crab, an invasive species, on the coastal ecosystems of North America. They found that these crabs significantly reduce the population of bivalves, such as native clams and oysters, through their voracious appetite. The green crabs also disrupt the habitat of other marine organisms by burrowing into the sediment and uprooting eelgrass beds. This destruction of eelgrass habitats has far-reaching consequences, as these areas serve as nurseries for various fish and crustacean species. Additionally, the crabs' activities have been observed to increase water turbidity and alter sediment composition. Some native predator populations have shown changes in their foraging patterns since the green crab invasion.

According to the text, how do European green crabs affect the broader coastal ecosystem?

A) They may trigger changes that the marine food chain by reducing more native clam populations than oyster populations.

B) Their burrowing behavior could gradually reshape the coastal seafloor, leading to widespread habitat changes for various species.

C) The destruction of eelgrass beds harms young fish and crustaceans by initiating changes in predator foraging patterns.

D) Their aggressive feeding habits may force native species to adapt their behavior, possibly leading to new interspecies relationships.

10

Pre-historic Artifacts Excavated in Mesopotamia

Artifact	Date of Content	Year of Discovery	Description
Warka Vase	3200-3000 BCE	1940	Carved alabaster vessel
Copper Bull	2600 BCE	1923	Copper sculpture
Standard of Ur	2600-2400 BCE	1920	Decorated wooden box
Mask of Warka	3100 BCE	1939	Marble face mask
Cylinder of Nabonidus	555-540 BCE	1854	Inscribed clay cylinder

Mesopotamia, an ancient region located in modern-day Iraq, has been a rich source of archaeological discoveries for centuries. Scholars have studied these artifacts to gain insights into the religious beliefs, social structures, and artistic traditions of the Sumerian, Akkadian, Babylonian, and Assyrian civilizations that once thrived in this area. While many significant finds were made in the 19th century, providing a treasure trove of information about the past, archaeologists have continued to uncover remarkable artifacts from various periods of Mesopotamian history throughout the 20th century. For instance, _____

Which choice most effectively uses data from the table to complete the statement?

A) the Standard of Ur, a decorated box, was the earliest discovered artifact in the 20th century, while the oldest artifact listed in the table, the Cylinder of Nabonidus, was found in 1854.

B) the Warka Vase, a carved alabaster vessel unearthed in 1940, and the Copper Bull, a copper sculpture from 2600 BCE discovered earlier in 1923, represent over 400 years of early Mesopotamian history.

C) the Warka Vase, crafted between 3200-3000 BCE was found in 1939, just one year before the discovery of the the Mask of Warka, dated around 3100 BCE.

D) the Mask of Warka, a marble face mask, was discovered in 1939, while the the Copper Bull, a copper statute, predating the mask by at least 500 years of Mesopotamian history was discovered in 1923.

11

World Coffee Production by Country (in thousand 60kg bags)

Country	2015	2016	2017	2018	2019
Brazil	50,388	51,000	51,500	50,000	58,000
Vietnam	26,500	25,000	28,500	30,000	31,000
Colombia	12,716	14,000	13,500	13,000	14,000
Indonesia	11,000	10,000	10,500	10,000	11,000
Ethiopia	6,400	6,500	6,800	7,600	7,500

Coffee is one of the most widely traded agricultural commodities in the world, with millions of farmers in developing countries relying on it for their livelihoods. The table above shows the coffee production data for the top five producing countries from 2015 to 2019. Upon analyzing the data, an economist claims that _____

Which choice most effectively uses data from the table to complete the economist's claim?

A) Vietnam's coffee production increased by 4,500 thousand 60kg bags between 2015 and 2019, the second-largest increase after Brazil.

B) Ethiopia's coffee production in 2019 was higher than Indonesia's production in 2015, despite Ethiopia being the smallest producer among the five countries.

C) Colombia's coffee production fluctuated the least among the five countries, with a difference of only 1,284 thousand 60kg bags between its highest and lowest production years.

D) Brazil's coffee production in 2016 was lower than its production in 2015, while all other countries showed an increase in production during the same period.

12

The Necklace is an 1884 short story by Guy de Maupassant. In the story, the narrator suggests that Mathilde Loisel is more affected by her surrounding than others are.

Which quotation from *The Necklace* most effectively illustrates this claim?

A) "She was one of those pretty and charming girls born, as though fate had blundered over her, into a family of artisans."

B) "She suffered from the poverty of her dwelling, from the worn walls, the abraded chairs, the ugliness of the stuffs. All these things, which another woman of her caste would not even have noticed, tortured her and made her indignant."

C) "She had no clothes, no jewels, nothing. And she loved nothing else; she felt herself made for that only. She would so much have liked to please, to be envied, to be seductive and sought after."

D) "She came to know the drudgery of housework, the odious labors of the kitchen. She washed the dishes, using her rosy nails upon the greasy pots and the bottoms of the stewpans."

Edenbrook Test 3

13

In a 2018 study, evolutionary biologist Dr. Sarah Thompson and her colleagues investigated the emergence of sexual dimorphism, the distinct differences in appearance between males and females of the same species. The team analyzed data from 1,000 bird species and observed a strong correlation between the degree of sexual dimorphism and the intensity of sexual selection pressures. Species with highly dimorphic traits often exhibited complex mating rituals and fierce competition for mates. Conversely, in species where sexual selection appeared less intense, the physical differences between males and females were typically less pronounced. Based on these findings, the team hypothesized that sexual dimorphism most likely _____

Which choice most logically completes the text?

A) evolved to facilitate species identification among the 1,000 bird species studied.

B) resulted from an interplay between genetic factors and environmental pressures across diverse habitats.

C) emerged as a consequence of evolutionary processes driven by mate choice and intrasexual competition.

D) arose to enhance the physical differences between males and females in species with complex mating systems.

14

Recent geological studies in the Badlands region revealed intricate formation patterns. Dr. Emily Sanders' team analyzed soil layers, finding evidence of both gradual erosion and abrupt changes. They observed fine sediment deposits suggesting wind activity during warm periods, alongside water-carved channels from cooler eras. Intriguingly, the most distinct landscape features corresponded to transitional climate phases. Volcanic ash traces were found sporadically throughout the layers, with variations in concentration indicating episodic volcanic activity. The team also noted irregularities in sedimentary structures that aligned with shifts in regional tectonic activity. Given these indings, the researchers concluded that the Badlands landscape formation _____

Which choice most logically completes the text?

A) primarily resulted from continuous wind-driven erosion with periodic volcanic ash deposits and regional tectonic shifts.

B) was shaped by a combination of gradual processes, including wind and water erosion, with significant contributions from episodic volcanic activity and tectonic movements.

C) occurred through alternating cycles of rapid water erosion, sediment accumulation, and localized volcanic events, with minimal influence from tectonic activity.

D) was predominantly influenced by volcanic activity, with episodic climate-driven erosion and minor tectonic adjustments playing a secondary role.

15

Urban planners have long sought ways to reduce traffic congestion in cities. Recently, a study of 20 major urban areas found that cities with extensive bike lane networks experienced significantly lower rates of traffic congestion during peak hours compared to cities with few or no bike lanes. Researchers studied the introduction of new bike lanes in five cities and found that for every mile of bike lane added, there was an average 3% reduction in cars on the road during rush hour. One potential explanation for this result is that the presence of bike lanes encourages many commuters to switch from driving to cycling, thereby reducing the number of cars on the road.

Which finding from the study, if true, would most directly weaken the potential explanation?

A) The reduction in car traffic was most pronounced in neighborhoods where new bike lanes were installed.

B) Traffic data showed that the decrease in car volume on roads with new bike lanes was offset by increased traffic on parallel routes without bike lanes.

C) Cities with new bike lanes also saw an increase in the use of electric scooters and other alternative transportation methods.

D) The decrease in car traffic was observed almost immediately after the bike lanes were installed, before cycling rates had significantly increased.

16

For years, researchers at Stanford University had studied the dwarf planet Ceres. The researchers did not find any major _____ each day was a repeat of yesterday. Just as they decided to shutter the program, an intern accidentally discovered a hidden pattern that would revolutionize our understanding of planetary formation.

Which choice completes the text so that it conforms to the conventions of Standard English?

A) revelations, however;
B) revelations, however,
C) revelations; however,
D) revelations. However,

17

On September 15, 1940, a British fighter plane called the Spitfire landed at RAF Tangmere _____ taken off from Duxford airbase under the command of Squadron Leader Douglas Bader and his wingman, Flight Lieutenant Hugh Dundas, a mere 47 minutes earlier, the legendary aircraft completed a crucial intercept mission that would be remembered for decades to come.

Which choice completes the text so that it conforms to the conventions of Standard English?

A) airfield and having
B) airfield having
C) airfield, having
D) airfield; having

18

A recent study monitored the diversity of coral species in thirty-five Great Barrier Reef locations over a fifteen-year period. Marine biologist and _____ a pioneer in reef restoration, discovered that when water temperatures in an area increased, the number of distinct coral species thriving in that location diminished.

Which choice completes the text so that it conforms to the conventions of Standard English?

A) conservationist Dr. Michael Chen

B) conservationist, Dr. Michael Chen,

C) conservationist Dr. Michael Chen,

D) conservationist, Dr. Michael Chen

19

Campaign finance reform has been a hot-button issue in modern politics, with many calling for stricter regulations on political donations and spending. In the realm of politics, voters would nonetheless benefit from the existence of a regulated campaign finance system, as many candidates would be _____ at least by a desire to avoid public backlash—to comply with the established rules and regulations.

Which choice completes the text so that it conforms to the conventions of Standard English?

A) motivated—if not by a sense of integrity—

B) motivated—if not by a sense of integrity,

C) motivated. If not by a sense of integrity,

D) motivated, if not by a sense of integrity—

20

In the field of economics, the term "intrapreneur" has been appropriately ascribed to individuals who operate within an existing organizational structure, _____ their extensive understanding of the firm's core competencies and resources, and use innovative strategies to create value for their organization and its stakeholders.

Which choice completes the text so that it conforms to the conventions of Standard English?

A) leveraging

B) leveraged

C) to leverage

D) leverage

21

The museum showcased various artifacts from ancient civilizations, including pottery, jewelry, and weaponry. Among these treasures _____ an intricately carved golden scepter with 12 rubies that drew the most attention from visitors

Which choice completes the text so that it conforms to the conventions of Standard English?

A) were

B) are

C) was

D) being

22

In the 3rd century BCE, contemplating the buoyancy of objects immersed in fluids, _____ would be equal to the weight of the fluid displaced by the object, a principle that later became known as Archimedes' principle.

Which choice completes the text so that it conforms to the conventions of Standard English?

A) the upward force was postulated by Archimedes that it

B) the postulate by Archimedes suggested that the upward force

C) Archimedes' postulate suggested that the upward force

D) Archimedes postulated that the upward force

23

In American football, the offensive team typically aims to advance the ball down the field by gaining yards through a series of plays, with the ultimate goal of scoring a touchdown. _____ in European football (soccer), the objective is to maintain possession of the ball, strategically maneuvering it across the pitch until an opportunity arises to score a goal by kicking the ball into the opposing team's net.

Which choice completes the text with the most logical transition?

A) On the one hand,

B) For example,

C) In addition,

D) Conversely,

24

The new technology promises to revolutionize the industry, offering faster and more efficient solutions. _____ implementing these changes will require significant investment, but the long-term benefits are undeniable.

Which choice completes the text with the most logical transition?

A) In contrast,

B) As a result,

C) That being said,

D) In the final analysis,

25

While researching a topic, a student has taken the following notes:

- A study by the Pew Research Center found that 72% of Americans use at least one social media platform.
- Social media allows users to connect with friends and family, share content, and express themselves.
- Research by psychologist Sherry Turkle suggests that social media can lead to decreased face-to-face communication and empathy.
- A survey by Common Sense Media found that 50% of teens feel addicted to their mobile devices and that 35% of teens prefer texting over in-person communication for serious conversations.
- A study by the University of Missouri found that social media can help introverted individuals form and maintain relationships.
- Social media has also been used to raise awareness about social issues and organize activism efforts.

The student wants to highlight a negative consequence of social media use on interpersonal communication. Which choice most effectively uses relevant information from the notes to accomplish this goal?

A) While social media can negatively impact face-to-face communication and empathy, it also helps introverted individuals form and maintain relationships.

B) 72% of Americans use at least one social media platform, allowing them to connect with friends and family, share content, and express themselves.

C) With a significant portion of teens preferring texting over in-person conversations for serious topics, social media use can lead to a decrease in face-to-face communication and empathy.

D) Psychologist Sherry Turkle indicates that social media use leads to a complete lack of face-to-face communication and empathy among users.

26

While researching a topic, a student has taken the following notes:

- Electric vehicles (EVs) produce zero direct emissions, reducing air pollution and greenhouse gas emissions.
- EVs are more energy-efficient than conventional gasoline-powered vehicles, converting up to 77% of electrical energy into power.
- The initial cost of purchasing an EV is generally higher than that of a comparable gasoline-powered vehicle.
- EVs have a limited driving range compared to gasoline-powered vehicles, typically between 100 and 300 miles per charge.
- As battery technology improves and production scales up, the cost of EVs is expected to decrease in the coming years.

The student wants to emphasize the environmental benefits of electric vehicles. Which choice most effectively uses relevant information from the notes to accomplish this goal?

A) The limited driving range and lack of charging infrastructure in rural areas can cause range anxiety for electric vehicle owners, potentially hindering widespread adoption.

B) Electric vehicles are more energy-efficient than gasoline-powered vehicles, converting up to 77% of electrical energy into power.

C) While the initial cost of purchasing an electric vehicle is higher than that of a comparable gasoline-powered vehicle, the cost is expected to decrease as battery technology improves and production scales up.

D) Electric vehicles produce zero direct emissions, which can help reduce air pollution and greenhouse gas emissions.

27

While researching a topic, a student has taken the following notes:

- Social media algorithms create "echo chambers" where users are exposed to ideas that align with their beliefs.
- 55% of U.S. adults get their news from social media, raising concerns about misinformation and fake news.
- Social media allows politicians to directly reach their audience, potentially increasing polarization.
- A study suggested that social media use does not necessarily lead to increased polarization due to exposure to diverse viewpoints.
- Social media has facilitated political mobilization and allowed marginalized groups to have a voice.

The student wants to argue that social media contributes to political polarization by enabling the spread of extreme views. Which choice most effectively uses relevant information from the notes to accomplish this goal?

A) The personalized nature of social media algorithms creates "echo chambers" that can reinforce existing beliefs and increase political polarization.

B) While social media can contribute to polarization, it has also been recognized for facilitating political mobilization and giving marginalized groups a platform.

C) A study suggested that social media use does not necessarily increase polarization, as users are exposed to diverse viewpoints through their networks.

D) While social media platforms have become a popular way for politicians to communicate with their constituents, 55% of U.S. adults get their news from social media.

STOP

TEST 3 ANSWER KEY

MODULE 1			MODULE 2		
1. B	10. B	19. B	1. A	10. B	19. B
2. C	11. B	20. C	2. C	11. A	20. D
3. C	12. D	21. C	3. B	12. B	21. C
4. A	13. D	22. B	4. A	13. C	22. D
5. A	14. C	23. D	5. C	14. B	23. D
6. C	15. D	24. C	6. D	15. D	24. C
7. D	16. C	25. B	7. B	16. A	25. C
8. D	17. D	26. A	8. A	17. D	26. D
9. C	18. B	27. A	9. B	18. C	27. A

To calculate your score, tally up the total number of correct answers from both Module 1 and Module 2. This is your RAW SCORE. Find your raw score below and your scaled score range is on the right.

Module 1 _____ + Module 2 _____ = Total Raw _____ = SCORE RANGE _____

TEST 3 – RAW SCORE CONVERSION

RAW SCORE (TOTAL CORRECT)	SCORE RANGE	RAW SCORE (TOTAL CORRECT)	SCORE RANGE
54	800-800	27	450-500
53	790-800	26	440-500
52	780-800	25	430-490
51	770-790	24	420-480
50	750-780	23	410-470
49	730-770	22	400-460
48	720-760	21	390-450
47	710-750	20	380-440
46	700-740	19	370-430
45	690-730	18	360-420
44	670-710	17	350-410
43	650-700	16	340-400
42	630-680	15	330-390
41	610-660	14	320-380
40	590-640	13	310-370
39	570-620	12	300-360
38	560-610	11	290-350
37	550-600	10	280-340
36	540-590	9	270-330
35	530-580	8	260-320
34	520-570	7	250-310
33	510-560	6	240-300
32	500-550	5	230-290
31	490-540	4	220-280
30	480-530	3	210-270
29	470-520	2	200-260
28	460-510	1	200-250

TEST 3: MODULE 1 ANSWER EXPLANATIONS

1. **Answer: B. Vocab in context.** The clues are *harmonizing* and *complementing,* which both connote a blending and interacting with the environment to create a *gentle symphony.* While the wind may be forming a sound, The winds are not *formed through the rustling leaves;* eliminate Choice A. Eliminate Choice C; the wind is not trying to escape the leaves. Eliminate Choice D; the word interlocked suggests a rigid connection, whereas the passage suggests a more gentle and fluid movement.

2. **Answer: C. Sentence completion.** The clues are *leading many to shut down* and *significantly reduce their workforce.* This means that the regulations have made it harmful. The word that comes closest in meaning is **prohibitive**, which means preventing something from occurring. Eliminate Choice A; **imperative** means urgent. Eliminate Choice B; **misconstrued** means misinterpreted. Eliminate Choice D; **conducive** means making an outcome more likely.

3. **Answer: C. Sentence completion.** The clue is *the atmosphere in the auditorium was electric.* Since the two rivals are ready to debate and the atmosphere was highly charged, we can logically complete the sentence with the word NOTICEABLE. The word that comes closest is meaning is **palpable**, which means able to be felt. Eliminate Choice A; **imperceptible** means not noticeable. Eliminate Choice B; **insignificant** contradicts the idea in the passage. Eliminate Choice D; **pretentious** means fake.

4. **Answer: A. Sentence completion.** The clues are *had little bearing* and *ultimately detracted,* meaning the information was unnecessary. The word that comes closest in meaning is **superfluous,** which means unnecessary. Eliminate Choice B; **paramount** means important. Eliminate Choice C; **pertinent** means relevant. Eliminate Choice D; succinct refers to speech or writing that is short and to the point.

5. **Answer: A. Sentence completion.** The clue is *solidifying her position as one of the most influential.* This means that she earned praise from her critics. The word that comes closest in meaning is **acclaim**, which means enthusiastic approval or praise. Eliminate Choice B; **repudiation** means a rejection. Eliminate Choice C; **ambivalence** means having mixed feelings. Eliminate Choice D; **prevalence** means being widespread or common.

6. **Answer: C. Global.** Use process of elimination. Eliminate Choice A; while technological advancements may have played a role, they are not mentioned or emphasized in this passage. Eliminate Choice B; there is no comparison. Eliminate Choice D; there is no advocacy for funding or resources. The opening sentence directly states that microfossil discovery has *revolutionized our understanding of early life on Earth.* Dr. Rodriguez then describes microfossils as providing *a window into ecosystems that existed billions of years ago.* The passage concludes by explaining that studying microfossils allows scientists to *piece together the story of how life evolved and adapted to Earth's changing conditions over vast stretches of time.* The *story* connects to **narrative.**

7. **Answer: D. Global.** Use process of elimination. Eliminate Choice A; it focuses only on one aspect—healing. Eliminate Choice B; it is too limited and doesn't capture the full range of contradictions. Eliminate Choice C; the confident tone of the poem negates the suggestion of an internal struggle. Notice how each stanza presents pairs of opposites or complementary ideas: Sorrow/grief and ending of grief; Beginning (bud) and end (late-falling leaf); Servant (serf) and ruler (king); Causing tears and curing tears; Dark and light physical features. The speaker claims to embody multiple, often contradictory, aspects of existence and experience. Moreover, the title *The Paradox* further emphasizes the theme of contradiction and complexity, supporting Choice D.

8. **Answer: D. Function.** To determine the function of the last sentence in the context of the whole poem, let's analyze the text: 1) The poem describes a dance performance, focusing on the dancer's movements and their expressive power. 2) Throughout the poem, the author uses vivid imagery to capture the essence of the dance. 3) The last sentence reads: *Defying gravity, embracing the night*. Now, use process of elimination. Eliminate Choice A; while the poem does describe the dancer's movements, the last line doesn't specifically emphasize technical difficulty. Eliminate Choice B; there is no indication about the temporary, or fleeting, nature of the performance. Eliminate Choice C; the line suggests overcoming limitations rather than struggling against them. Choice D works best as *Defying gravity* underscores the exceptional skill of the dancer, while *embracing the night* implies artistry and perhaps a connection with something deeper or more mysterious.

9. **Answer: C. Global.** Notice that each answer choice has two parts. Evaluate the merits of both parts. Use process of elimination. Choice A is accurate in describing the initial setting establishment but inaccurate in characterizing the subsequent focus as being on the character's emotions. Choice B is inaccurate in both parts, as the text neither primarily presents the character's actions nor explains reasons behind actions. Choice D is inaccurate in both parts, as the text does not portray memories or contrast them with the current situation. Choice C is accurate on both accounts. **Character's reflections** = *thinking about things* and **character's observations** = *I could see…*

10. **Answer: B. Detail.** Connect the question stem to the excerpt: **what did Charles Darwin study during his voyage** = *voyage on the HMS Beagle, during which he studied the diverse flora and fauna of various regions*. Eliminate Choice A; this is his proposed theory, not the object of study during his voyage. Eliminate Choice C; this uses an unnecessary comparative that states **flora > fauna**. Eliminate D; this is quite possible, but it is not explicitly stated. Notice the link: **variety** = *diverse*, **plant and animal** = *flora and fauna*.

11. **Answer: B. Supporting claims.** Identify the claim to support: *scientists operate within a prevailing paradigm until anomalies arise that cannot be explained by the current framework*. Eliminate Choice A; it merely describes how **normal science** operates. Eliminate Choice C; this is a very close distractor as it suggests that new paradigms are always compared with the existing paradigm before settling on the matter. However, it lacks the reference to *anomalies*. Eliminate Choice D; this is about the age of the people who develop new paradigms. Choice B best supports the claim; link **empirical incongruities** = *anomalies*, **foundational premises of their established frames** = *prevailing paradigm…current framework*, **reexamine** = *operate until …*

12. **Answer: D. Weakening claims.** First identify the hypothesis: *mussels…were removing large amounts of phytoplankton and other suspended particles from the water column, thus increasing water clarity.* Eliminate Choice A; this weakens the secondary observation about the plant and algae proliferation, but it has no impact on the core hypothesis linking mussels and water clarity. Eliminate Choice B; the population differences between invasive and native mussels have no bearing on water clarity; Eliminate Choice C; this, again, is irrelevant. The impact on water clarity is missing. Choice D makes it clear that the mussels may not be the causal factor leading to increased water clarity; This contradictory result in a different setting suggests that zebra mussels may not be the primary causal factor for water clarity changes, as their presence doesn't consistently lead to the hypothesized outcome across various lake ecosystems.

13. **Answer: D. Logical completion.** Identify the line of reasoning: 1)Previous research shows that insect species with narrow geographical ranges tend to be more genetically homogeneous than those with extensive ranges. 2) Researchers simulated what would happen if B. affinis spread to new habitats outside its current range. 3) If the results should be consistent with previous findings, then increasing the range should increase diversity. Eliminate Choice A; it overgeneralizes by making a claim about the entire species rather than the specific species. Eliminate Choice B; it specifies the correct species, but contradicts previous findings; the homogeneity should decrease. Eliminate Choice C; this contradicts previous findings; the diversity should increase. Choice D is consistent with previous findings that increasing geographical ranges should lead to less genetic homogeneity, or increased diversity.

14. **Answer: C. Infographic & supporting claims.** First, identify the claim to support: *the frequency of mentions and the popularity index in literature reflect the cultural importance and popularity of these foods in English society during the studied period.* Next evaluate each choice based on accuracy and relevance. Effectively rule out answer choices that cannot satisfy both conditions.

    A) Relevant but inaccurate: Roast beef does have the second-highest popularity index at 37, behind tea at 92. However, it confuses the year mentioned with the frequency.
    B) Relevant but inaccurate: Tea has 2036 mentions, the highest of any food item. However, its first year of mention is 1390, not 1657.
    C) Relevant and accurate: Numbers for both Tea and Bread Pudding are accurate. Relevant: The contrast of the highest and the lowest along with their corresponding popularity index supports the main claim.
    D) Accurate but irrelevant: The figures are correct. However, it fails to demonstrate relevance to the claim: it focuses only on two low-ranking items without showing that the frequency of mention counts relate to their popularity indices.

15. **Answer: D. Punctuation.** First, eliminate Choice A and C. The sentence begins as a declarative (regular sentence) not a question mark. Then, notice that the words in Choice B is organized in a question form (*how was that power achieved*). Choice D properly organizes the words as a sentence and ends with a period.

16. **Answer: C. Punctuation.** The word *would* is a predicate verb so it must connect to a subject noun. The only choices that allow you to do that is A (**Anyone**...*would be wise*) and C. (***Anyone interested in starting a 3D printing business*** *would be wise*). Both are grammatically correct, but *interested in starting a 3D printing business* is essential as not ANYONE, but ANYONE INTERESTED IN 3D would be wise to work with others. Since that phrase is essential, you must remove the commas.

17. **Answer: D. Subject-verb.** The answer choices must connect to its subject noun, which is *A recent study*. Since it's singular, the subject noun must take the singular verb **presents**. Also notice that Choice D is the only singular.

    A) have presented – plural
    B) presenting – neither
    C) present – plural
    D) presents – singular

    If you have no idea, it's usually the odd man out between singular and plural verbs.

18. **Answer: B. IDP and punctuation.** Notice the semi-colon in choice A. Examine the components to the left and right of the semi-colon. You will notice that the left contains a dependent clause, so eliminate Choice A. An independent clause must occupy the left of the semi-colon. Now, notice to the right of the word **lights**, there is a full independent clause. This means that the word *seem* must connect to **K-pop idols**. Eliminate Choice C, since the comma disconnects the two. Now, notice the difference between Choices B and D. The difference is the comma. Since there is a subordinate clause (*As they dance...lights*) before the independent clause (**the K-pop idols...***photographed*), there needs to be a comma. Eliminate Choice D.

19. **Answer: B. Punctuation.** Here, you need to understand the word **or** is being used to provide clarifying information. When you use the word "or" as a clarifier, you need a comma before that. Like this: The Big Mac, or McDonald's most popular burger, is delicious. Notice that *or McDonald's most popular burger* is otherwise known as the Big Mac. In such cases, you need to bracket up the clarifying information with commas. Without the commas, as in Choice A, the word *or* serves to highlight two different things: Physics or Chemistry is taken by sophomores. Notice here, the *or* is connecting two distinct objects. Eliminate Choice A. Choice C unnecessarily brackets the extra info with an asymmetrical dash and comma. Choice D is missing the closing comma.

20. **Answer: C. IDP.** Break up the sentence into independent, dependent, and phrase.

    A) [PHRASE]The research institutes' scientists, [DEPENDENT] many of whom have earned a doctoral degree in pharmacology or a related field and use cutting-edge laboratory equipment such as high performance liquid chromatography systems that isolate and characterize drug compounds.
    B) [PHRASE]The research institutes' scientists, [DEPENDENT] many of whom have earned a doctoral degree in pharmacology or a related field. [INDEPENDENT] They use cutting-edge laboratory equipment such as high performance liquid chromatography systems that isolate and characterize drug compounds.

C) [INDEPENDENT]The research institutes' scientists, [DEPENDENT] many of whom have earned a doctoral degree in pharmacology or a related field [/DEPENDENT], use cutting-edge laboratory equipment such as high performance liquid chromatography systems that isolate and characterize drug compounds.

D) [PHRASE]The research institutes' scientists, [DEPENDENT] many of whom have earned a doctoral degree in pharmacology or a related field. [INDEPENDENT] Moreover, they use cutting-edge laboratory equipment such as high performance liquid chromatography systems that isolate and characterize drug compounds.

Now examine the configurations with the punctuation.
A) P, D. = INVALID
B) P, D. I. = INVALID
C) I (with a nested dependent clause in between) = VALID
D) P, D. I. = INVALID

Choice A is invalid because it has no independent clause. Choice B and Choice D are invalid because the first construction that ends with a period contains no independent clause.

21. **Answer: C. Transitions.** Let's analyze the relationship between the two statements: The first statement introduces the blue whale as the largest animal known to have ever existed on Earth. The second statement provides specific information about the largest blue whale ever recorded, giving its length and estimated weight. The second statement supports and reinforces the first by providing concrete details. Now, let's consider each option.

    A) "Furthermore" - This would work, as it introduces additional information, but it's not the strongest choice.
    B) "In contrast" - This doesn't fit, as the second statement isn't contrasting with the first.
    C) "In fact" - This is the best choice, as it introduces specific evidence that supports and emphasizes the first statement.
    D) "On the other hand" - Like "in contrast," this doesn't work because the statements aren't opposing each other.

    The most logical transition is "in fact". This phrase is used to introduce a specific example or piece of evidence that supports or emphasizes a previous statement.

22. **Answer: B. Transitions.** Let's analyze the relationship between the two statements to determine the most logical transition: The first statement introduces Venus as Earth's "sister planet" due to similarities in size and composition. The second statement discusses scientists' interest in studying Venus to understand specific planetary phenomena. The second statement follows from the first, explaining a consequence or result of the similarity between Venus and Earth. It's not contrasting or providing an example, but rather showing how the similarity leads to scientific interest. Let's examine each option:

    A) "Nevertheless" - This doesn't fit, as it would imply a contrast or contradiction between the statements, which isn't present.

B) "Accordingly" - This is the best choice, as it indicates that the second statement logically follows from or is a result of the first.

C) "For instance" - This doesn't work here, as the second statement isn't providing a specific example of the first.

D) "Conversely" - This is inappropriate, as the second statement isn't presenting an opposite or contrasting idea.

The most logical transition is B) "accordingly". This word shows that the scientific interest in Venus is a logical consequence of its similarity to Earth. It connects the idea of Venus being Earth's "sister planet" to the resulting scientific curiosity about what we can learn from studying it.

23. **Answer: D. Transition.** Let's analyze the relationship between the statements to determine the most logical transition: The first statement presents a commonly cited claim about the Great Wall of China. The second statement directly contradicts this claim, calling it a misconception. The third part provides evidence supporting why it's a misconception. We need a transition that indicates a contrast or contradiction between the common belief and the factual information that follows. Let's examine each option:

A) "in addition" - This doesn't work because the following information isn't additional to the claim, but rather contradicts it.

B) "in fact" - While this could work to introduce contradictory information, it's not the best choice here as it doesn't clearly signal the contrast.

C) "in other words" - This isn't appropriate because the following information isn't restating the first claim in different words, but contradicting it.

D) "however" - This is the best choice as it clearly signals a contrast between the common belief and the factual information that follows.

The most logical transition is D) "however". This word effectively introduces the contradiction between the popular belief and the reality about the visibility of the Great Wall from space. It signals to the reader that the information following will challenge or contradict the initial statement.

24. **Answer: C. Transition.** Let's analyze the relationship between the two parts of this sentence: The first part describes the team's diligent practice and effort over weeks. The second part reveals that despite this preparation, they were outmatched in the championship game. We need a transition that shows a contrast between the team's preparation and the unexpected outcome of the game. Let's examine each option:

A) "in fact" - This doesn't work because the second part isn't elaborating on or confirming the first part, but rather presenting a contrasting outcome.

B) "specifically" - This isn't appropriate as the second part isn't providing a specific example of their practice, but rather an unexpected result.

C) "for all that" - This is the best choice as it indicates that despite the team's efforts, a different outcome occurred.

D) "additionally" - This doesn't fit because the second part isn't adding to the information about their practice, but presenting a contrasting result.

The most logical transition is "for all that". This phrase effectively conveys that despite the team's hard work and preparation (as described in the first part), they still found themselves outmatched in the game (as stated in the second part).

25. **Answer: B. Rhetorical synthesis.** Find the answer that supports the question stem: **contrast the relative sizes of the two organisms.** Eliminate Choice A; it discusses the two organisms' roles in the food chain. Eliminate Choice C; it discusses the two organisms' roles in the ecosystem. Eliminate Choice D; it discusses the phytoplankton's visibility from space and the copepod's importance as food. Choice B properly contains the two sizes (**2 to 200 meters…0.5 to 2 millimeters**).

26. **Answer: A. Rhetorical synthesis.** Find the answer that supports the question stem: **a disadvantage of electric cars.** Eliminate Choice B; it uses information from the second bullet point, which actually presents an advantage of electric cars, not a disadvantage. It's not suitable for explaining a disadvantage. Eliminate Choice C; while it mentions environmental damage and concerns, it combines this with a positive aspect (**zero direct emissions**). The combination makes it less effective in clearly presenting a disadvantage. Eliminate Choice D; similar to Choice C, it mixes advantages and disadvantages. While it mentions indirect contribution to pollution, it starts with the positive aspect of reducing urban air pollution, which dilutes the focus on the disadvantage.

27. **Answer: A. Rhetorical synthesis.** Find the answer that supports the question stem: summarize the results of the study. Eliminate B; it discusses the methodology. Eliminate C; it discusses the aim and the goal of the study. Eliminate D; it discusses a limitation. Choice A summarizes the data and the results from the experiment.

TEST 3: MODULE 2 ANSWER EXPLANATIONS

1. **Answer: A. Sentence completion.** The clues are *seemed sufficiently* and *However, the company*. This suggests that it was better to reconsider the sufficiency of the prototype. Therefore, the company would think that it's best or wise to halt the project. The word **prudent** means wise. Eliminate Choice B; **derelict** means in a poor and neglected condition (or as a noun a person without a home or property). Eliminate Choice C; **pernicious** means harmful. Eliminate Choice D; **indifferent** means having no interest or care.

2. **Answer: C. Sentence completion.** The clue is *lacking substance* and *mislead*, which suggests that the arguments were false or deceptive. The word that matches most closely is **spurious**, which means fake or false. Eliminate Choice A; **coherent** means logical and consistent. Eliminate Choice B; **succinct** means short and clearly expressed in speech. Eliminate Choice D; **dilatory** means slow to act or late.

3. **Answer: B. Sentence completion.** The clue is *act of defiance* and *establish a new, just system*. Taken together, the rebels would want to destroy the existing government. The word that comes closest in meaning is **topple**, which means to overthrow. Eliminate Choice A; **delegate** means to assign. Eliminate Choice C; **renounce** means to reject or to abandon. Eliminate Choice D; **invalidate** means to make (usually an argument) unsound or fallacious. Note that invalidate refers primarily to arguments, so invalidating the government may feel right, but the sense is a bit off.

4. **Answer: A. Sentence completion.** The clue is *leaving nothing*. The word that comes closest in meaning is **raze**, which means to destroy. Eliminate Choice B; **remonstrate** means to protest. Eliminate Choice C; **recapitulate** means to summarize and conclude. Eliminate Choice D; **reprove** means to scold.

5. **Answer: C. Cross-text.** First identify the argument of the **critics** in Text 1: *critics contend that this method is speculative and risks imposing modern biases, leading to ethnocentric interpretations*. Notice here that *this method* refers to *reconstruct ancient technical choices, social structures, and cultural norms*. Now, identify the line that discusses this in Text 2. You can connect *reconstruct* in text one to *recreate* in Text 2: *the limitations of the archaeological record and the inability to fully recreate past contexts may lead to unwarranted speculation, necessitating a reflexive and multivocal approach to archaeological hermeneutics*. Notice here that the answer is *necessitating a reflexive and multivocal approach*. Eliminate Choice A; Text 2 actually disagrees. Eliminate Choice B; Choice B is partially correct as it acknowledges the valuable insights gained from experimental archaeology, which Text 2 indeed emphasizes. However, it overstates the sufficiency of these insights to counter critics' concerns, ignoring Text 2's explicit recognition of limitations and its suggestion for a more nuanced, reflexive approach to address the issues raised by critics. Eliminate Choice D; Text 2 disagrees, but its concession to some of its benefits cannot support **strongly disagree.**

6. **Answer: D. Function.** Sentence 1 introduces an example of *juvenilia*. Sentence 2 defines *juvenilia* and explains its growing appeal (*more and more popular*). Sentence 3 explains the possible causes for its popularity. Eliminate Choice A; while Sentence 2 introduces its significance, Sentence 1

introduces Carroll's work. Eliminate Choice B; again, the example is in Sentence 1. Eliminate Choice C; there's no indication within the sentence that it was unpopular.

7. **Answer: B. Global.** Use process of elimination. Eliminate Choice A; this option focuses on a specific detail from the study rather than capturing the main idea of the passage. Eliminate Choice C; this answer overstates the certainty of climate change impacts and focuses on a potential future implication rather than the primary finding of the study about soil temperature's role in cicada emergence. Eliminate Choice D; this option incorrectly states that the study's findings could alter cicada emergence timing, when in fact the study discovered the existing trigger for emergence, and it's climate change that might potentially alter the timing in the future.

8. **Answer: A. Global.** Use process of elimination. Eliminate Choice B; this choice mischaracterizes the interaction, as there's no indication of an argument between Dorothea and Will, and it incorrectly portrays Mr. Brooke's reaction. Eliminate Choice C; this option introduces elements not present in the text, such as Will professing his love, and misrepresents the emotional dynamics described. Eliminate Choice D; this choice incorrectly positions Mr. Brooke as the primary actor, when the passage focuses on Dorothea's emotional expression and its impact on others. Notice the links between the answer choice and the text: **uncharacteristic emotional openness** = *Dorothea… had forgotten everything except the relief of pouring forth her feelings* and **prompting a reassessment of perceptions** = *A man is seldom ashamed of feeling that he cannot love a woman so well when he sees a certain greatness in her.* In other words, Dorothea's honesty is forcing Will to reassess his opinion of her.

9. **Answer: B. Details.** First find the link between the question stem to the excerpt: **European green crabs affect the <u>broader</u> coastal ecosystem** = *This destruction of eelgrass habitats has <u>far-reaching</u> consequences, as these areas serve as nurseries for various fish and crustacean species. Additionally, the crabs' activities have been observed to increase water turbidity and alter sediment composition.* The link is **broader** and *far-reaching*. From there, notice that *destruction of eelgrass habitats…increase water turbidity and alter sediment composition* = **gradually reshape the coastal seafloor** and *widespread habitat changes for various species* = **nurseries for various fish and crustacean species.** Eliminate Choice A; while the text mentions that green crabs reduce bivalve populations, it doesn't specifically compare their impact on clams versus oysters or discuss broader changes to the marine food chain. Eliminate Choice C; although the text mentions destruction of eelgrass beds and changes in predator foraging patterns, it doesn't directly link these two effects or suggest that changes in predator behavior harm young fish and crustaceans.
Eliminate Choice D; the text doesn't mention native species adapting their behavior or new interspecies relationships forming as a result of the green crabs' presence.

10. **Answer: B. Infographic and supporting claims.** First, identify the claim to support: *archaeologists have continued to uncover remarkable artifacts from various periods of Mesopotamian history throughout the 20th century.* Next, use process of elimination. Eliminate Choice A; the inclusion of an artifact in 1854 references the 19th century, not the 20th. Eliminate Choice C; the Warka Vase was found in 1940, not 1939. Eliminate Choice D; the Copper Bull was discovered in 2600 BCE and the Mask of Warka was discovered in 3100 BCE. The answer choice says that the Copper Bull *predates*; it's the other way around: the Mask of Warka predates the Copper Bull. Choice B accurately supports

the claim that artifacts (the Warka Vase and the Copper Bull) were discovered in the 20th century (1940 and 1923, respectively).

11. **Answer: A. Infographics.** Use process of elimination. Eliminate Choice B; it is inaccurate since Ethiopia was lower than Indonesia. Eliminate Choice C; to determine **fluctuation** subtract the highest and lowest production years. Columbia (1,284), Brazil (8,000), Vietnam (6,000), Indonesia (1,000), Ethiopia (1,100). Indonesia fluctuates the least. Eliminate Choice D; Brazil increased 50,388; 2016: 51,000. In addition, Vietnam and Indonesia decreased from 2015 to 2016, contradicting the claim. Choice A is the only accurate choice; Vietnam's production: 2019 (31,000) - 2015 (26,500) = 4,500 and Brazil's increase: 58,000 - 50,388 = 7,612, which is indeed larger. This is correct and matches the data.

12. **Answer: B. Supporting claims.** First, identify the claim to exemplify: *Mathilde Loisel is more affected by her surrounding than others are.* Use process of elimination. Eliminate Choice A; this quote introduces Mathilde and suggests that she doesn't fit into her social class. It implies that she was meant for a higher station in life but was mistakenly born into a working-class family, hinting at her dissatisfaction. Eliminate Choice C; this quote describes Mathilde's desires and her belief that she was meant for a life of luxury and admiration. It shows her longing for material possessions and social status, focusing more on her internal desires rather than her reaction to her environment. Eliminate Choice D; this quote describes Mathilde's experience with household chores, emphasizing how unpleasant she finds them. The contrast between her "rosy nails" and the "greasy pots" highlights her perceived mismatch with her current situation. For Choice B, note that **"She suffered from the poverty of her dwelling"**=*affected by her surrounding* and **"All these things, which another woman of her caste would not even have noticed"**=*than others are.*

13. **Answer: C. Logical completion.** First, identify the line of reasoning. 1) The excerpt describes a study that found a strong correlation between sexual dimorphism and sexual selection pressures in bird species. 2) Species with more pronounced sexual dimorphism showed more intense sexual selection (complex mating rituals, fierce competition for mates). 3) Conversely, species with less intense sexual selection had less pronounced physical differences between sexes. The logical conclusion here must explain the relationship between sexual selection and the development of sexual dimorphism. Use process of elimination. Eliminate Choice A; the study's findings relate sexual dimorphism to mating behavior, not to distinguishing between different species. Eliminate Choice B; the study's findings relate sexual dimorphism to mating behavior, not to distinguishing between different species. Eliminate Choice D; this choice reverses the cause and effect relationship suggested by the study. The study implies that sexual dimorphism is a result of sexual selection pressures, not that it arose to enhance differences in species that already had complex mating systems. Choice C is the best answer because it suggests that the sexual dimorphism observed in the study is a result of evolutionary processes related to mating and competition

14. **Answer: B. Logical completion.** First, identify the line of reasoning. 1) The study found evidence of both gradual erosion and abrupt changes in the Badlands' soil layers, with wind and water activity linked to different climate periods. 2) Distinct landscape features corresponded to transitional climate phases, while volcanic ash traces indicated episodic volcanic activity. 3) Irregularities in sedimentary

structures aligned with shifts in regional tectonic activity, leading to a conclusion for the Badlands landscape formation. The answer choice must describe their conclusion based on the given observations. Use process of elimination. Eliminate Choice A; it overemphasizes wind-driven erosion as the primary factor. The excerpt mentions multiple factors, including water erosion, and doesn't indicate that wind erosion was the dominant process. Eliminate Choice C; it downplays the role of tectonic activity, which the excerpt specifically mentions as aligning with irregularities in sedimentary structures. It also overemphasizes rapid water erosion, while the excerpt mentions both gradual and abrupt changes. Eliminate Choice D; it overstates the importance of volcanic activity. While volcanic ash was found, it's described as "sporadic" and "episodic," not as the predominant influence. It also understates the role of climate-driven erosion and tectonic activity. Choice B is the best answer because it accurately reflects the complex interplay of factors described in the excerpt without overemphasizing one process over another: **gradual processes**=*erosion* and **episodic events**=*volcanic activity, tectonic movements*, both **wind and water erosion**=*wind...alongside water*, and **volcanic activity and tectonic movements**=*volcanic activity...tectonic activity*.

15. **Answer: D. Weakening claims.** First, identify the claim to weaken: *the presence of bike lanes encourages many commuters to switch from driving to cycling, thereby reducing the number of cars on the road.* Now, use process of elimination. Eliminate Choice A; this option actually strengthens the explanation rather than weakening it. If the reduction in car traffic is most noticeable where bike lanes were added, it supports the idea that the bike lanes are causing the change. This aligns with the hypothesis that people are switching from cars to bikes in areas where bike infrastructure is improved. Eliminate Choice B; while this option does weaken the overall claim that bike lanes reduce total traffic congestion, it doesn't directly weaken the specific explanation that people are switching from cars to bikes. Instead, it suggests that drivers are simply choosing different routes rather than changing their mode of transportation. Eliminate Choice C; this option introduces additional factors that could explain the reduction in car traffic, which does slightly weaken the bike lane explanation. However, it doesn't directly contradict the idea that people are switching from cars to alternative modes of transport. In fact, it could be seen as supporting the general concept that improving infrastructure for alternative transportation leads to less car use. Choice C suggests that the reduction in car traffic cannot be primarily attributed to people switching from cars to bicycles, as the effect was observed before there was a significant increase in cycling rates. This timing discrepancy directly challenges the proposed cause-and-effect relationship between increased bike lane availability and reduced car traffic due to modal shift.

16. **Answer: A. Punctuation.** First, eliminate Choices C and D since the only difference between the two is a period and a semi-colon. These can be eliminated right off the bat. Eliminate Choice B. This creates a comma splice. The adverbial *However* cannot combine two sentences with a comma. There should be a semi-colon or a period. Choice A, properly places the *however* in sentence number 2 so that it contrasts the *For years, ...* **However,** *did not find any major revelations.*

17. **Answer: D. Punctuation.** Start with the semi-colon. Notice to the left of the semi-colon, you have a full independent clause: *On September 15, 1940, a British fighter plane called the Spitfire landed at RAF Tangmere.* Now to the right of the semi-colon, you have a phrase (*taken off from Duxford airbase under the command of Squadron Leader Douglas Bader and his wingman, Flight Lieutenant*

Hugh Dundas, a mere 47 minutes earlier) followed by an independent clause (*the legendary aircraft completed a crucial intercept mission that would be remembered for decades to come*). No other answer choice contains a punctuation that allows for the combination of the two independent clauses. Now, choice A may work, but the word *and* needs a comma before it in order to complete the dependent clause: **John was happy, and he went dancing** is correct. **John was happy and he went dancing**, without the comma, is incorrect.

18. **Answer: C. Punctuation.** First, notice that it's testing the information associated with names. Look at the beginning of the sentence and notice that an article (a/an/the) is missing. This means that the information about Dr. Michael Chen is functions as a title. You do not need a comma for titles. Eliminate Choices B and D because they contain commas. Next, compare Choices A and C. Notice that the difference here is the comma after Dr. Michael Chen. Notice that to the right there is additional information (starting with the article *a*). This is additional information (fancy term being an appositive), which requires a comma sandwich around them. Eliminate Choice A.

19. **Answer: B. Punctuation.** Test Choice C first, since it contains a period. Notice that there is no sentence to the right of the period. Eliminate Choice C. Now, notice that they are testing the placement of dashes. Right below the blank is the closing dash. Eliminate Choice A since it would create three dashes. Now, eliminate Choice D because the last word before the dash and the first word after the dash should connect. Choice A creates *many candidates would be motivated…to comply with the established rules*. Choice D creates *if not by a sense of integrity…to comply with the rules*, which doesn't clarify the meaning of the sentence.

20. **Answer: D. Parallel structure.** Notice that there is a list of three things that describe *individuals who operate…, _____, and use*. The word leverage keeps the same parallel form as *operate* and *use*.

21. **Answer: C. Subject-verb.** This is an example of adverbial fronting. The subject is to the right of the verb. In regular syntax, we would say *an intricately carved golden* **scepter was** *among these treasures*.

22. **Answer: D. Modifier.** The modifier is *contemplating the buoyancy…*. The word that follows the comma after the modifier must be the object that is doing the contemplating. Choice D correctly starts with **Archimedes.**

23. **Answer: D. Transitions.** Let's analyze the relationship between the two sentences. The first sentence discusses an aspect about American football. The second sentence discusses an aspect of European football. The best transition, therefore, is **Conversely,** which serves to draw a contrast. Choice A's **On the one hand** is used to introduce a contrast and it must use "On the other hand" to draw the contrast. Choice B does not work because European football is not an example of American football. Choice C does not work because we are not adding more information about American football.

24. **Answer: C. Transitions.** Let's analyze the relationship between the two sentences. The first sentence talks about the promise of new technology to revolutionize the industry with faster and more efficient solutions. The second part of the sentence mentions that implementing these changes will require significant investment, but there are long-term benefits. Eliminate A. **In contrast** suggests that the second part contradicts the first, which isn't the case. The need for investment doesn't contrast with the benefits of the technology. **As a result** implies that the need for investment is a direct result of the technology's promise, which isn't quite accurate. **That being said** is used to introduce a contrasting or limiting statement. It acknowledges the positive aspects mentioned before while introducing a caveat or consideration. **In the final analysis,** is typically used to introduce a concluding statement or overall assessment, which doesn't fit well here as we're not concluding, but rather adding more information.

    The most logical transition here is C) "That being said,". It acknowledges the positive aspects of the new technology mentioned in the first sentence while introducing the caveat about the significant investment required.

25. **Answer: C. Rhetorical synthesis.** Find the answer that **highlights a negative consequence of social media use on interpersonal communication.** Eliminate Choice A; it presents both negative and positive aspects. Eliminate Choice B; it doesn't focus on negative consequences at all. Eliminate Choice D; it overstates Turkle's findings. Choice C effectively highlights a negative consequence by combining two relevant pieces of information from the notes: *35% of teens prefer texting over in-person communication for serious conversations* and *Research by psychologist Sherry Turkle suggests that social media can lead to decreased face-to-face communication and empathy*. This choice properly emphasizes the negative impact, as evidenced by the specific phrases: **With a significant portion of teens preferring texting over in-person conversations for serious topics** and **social media use can lead to a decrease in face-to-face communication and empathy**. This effectively synthesizes the information from the notes to highlight a specific negative consequence of social media on interpersonal communication.

26. **Answer: D. Rhetorical synthesis.** Find the answer that **emphasizes the environmental benefits of electric vehicles.** Eliminate Choice A; it focuses on limitations of EVs rather than environmental benefits. Eliminate Choice C; it discusses cost factors without addressing environmental impacts. Choice B mentions energy efficiency, which is related to environmental benefits, but doesn't directly address emissions or pollution. Choice D most effectively emphasizes environmental benefits, as evidenced by the specific phrases: **produce zero direct emissions** and **can help reduce air pollution and greenhouse gas emissions**. This directly corresponds to the note: *Electric vehicles (EVs) produce zero direct emissions, reducing air pollution and greenhouse gas emissions*. Choice D effectively synthesizes this information to highlight the primary environmental advantage of EVs, directly addressing the goal of emphasizing their environmental benefits.

27. **Answer: A. Rhetorical synthesis.** Find the answer that **argues that social media contributes to political polarization by enabling the spread of extreme views.** Eliminate Choice B; it presents both positive and negative aspects of social media in politics. Eliminate Choice C; it contradicts the goal by suggesting social media doesn't necessarily increase polarization. Eliminate Choice D; it

combines two unrelated points without directly addressing polarization. Choice A most effectively argues for social media's role in political polarization, as evidenced by the phrases: **personalized nature of social media algorithms creates "echo chambers"** and **can reinforce existing beliefs and increase political polarization**. This directly corresponds to the note: *Social media algorithms create "echo chambers" where users are exposed to ideas that align with their beliefs*. Choice A effectively synthesizes this information to highlight how social media's algorithmic nature can contribute to political polarization by limiting exposure to diverse viewpoints and potentially amplifying extreme opinions.

Reading and Writing

32 MINUTES, 27 QUESTIONS

DIRECTIONS

The questions in this section address a number of important reading and writing skills. Each question includes one or more passages, which may include a table or graph. Read each passage and question carefully, and then choose the best answer to the question based on the passage(s).

All questions in this section are multiple-choice with four answer choices. Each question has a single best answer.

1

Environmental scientists have long been _____ for stricter regulations on industrial emissions, citing compelling evidence that links air pollution to various respiratory diseases and climate change. Their research findings and persistent efforts have played a crucial role in shaping public opinion and influencing policy decisions at both national and international levels.

Which choice completes the text with the most logical and precise word or phrase?

A) advocating

B) rationalizing

C) deliberating

D) impeding

2

The Arctic is often portrayed in popular media as a vast, white wilderness of endless ice fields and barren, snow-covered landscapes, but in reality, its environment is far from _____, featuring a rich tapestry of diverse ecosystems ranging from tundra and boreal forests to complex marine environments teeming with unique life forms.

Which choice completes the text with the most logical and precise word or phrase?

A) homogenous

B) interdependent

C) prolific

D) trendy

3

The designs of Japanese architect Tadao Ando are _____ in prestigious buildings around the world, but the small residential projects he completed as a self-taught professional early in his career were constructed mainly in the streets of Osaka.

Which choice completes the text with the most logical and precise word or phrase?

A) contained
B) invented
C) adjusted
D) featured

4

The following text is adapted from a 19th century novel. The narrator is traveling in a foreign land.

> Our expedition was beset by every conceivable hardship that Nature, in her capricious cruelty, could devise. The rains fell with a ferocity heretofore unknown to civilized man, transforming the very earth beneath our feet into a quagmire of despair. Beasts of terrifying aspect lurked in the shadows, their baleful eyes glinting with predatory intent. Verily, it seemed as though Providence itself had conspired to thwart our noble endeavour.

As used in the text, what does the word "conceivable" most nearly mean?

A) Noticeable
B) Possible
C) Fanciful
D) Believable

5

The works of eighteenth-century German philosopher Immanuel Kant _____ those of other Enlightenment thinkers by replacing rationalist and empiricist traditions, while profoundly shaping subsequent philosophical discourse and laying the groundwork for modern Western philosophy.

Which choice completes the text with the most logical and precise word or phrase?

A) echoed
B) detained
C) supplemented
D) superseded

6

In the depths of the Pacific Ocean, hydrothermal vents spew superheated water laden with toxic chemicals into the surrounding cold seawater. Despite these harsh conditions, vibrant ecosystems thrive around these vents, fed by microbes that harness chemical energy from the vents. Dr. Sylvia Earle, a renowned marine biologist, has studied these unique oases of life to understand how organisms adapt to extreme environments. Her findings not only shed light on the resilience of life on Earth but also inform the search for extraterrestrial life on ocean worlds like Jupiter's moon Europa. <u>The discovery of these chemosynthetic ecosystems has expanded our understanding of the diverse conditions under which life can flourish, challenging long-held assumptions about the necessity of sunlight for sustaining life on Earth and beyond.</u>

Which choice best describes the function of the underlined sentence in the text as a whole?

A) To elaborate on the implications of the study's primary findings

B) To identify a possible limitation in the data used to support the conclusions of the study

C) To suggest possible avenue of future research in another discipline

D) To call into question the assumptions guiding the research

7

The International Olympic Committee (IOC) has introduced full-immersion virtual reality (VR) training programs for certain Olympic sports, including swimming and javelin throw. Athletes can use VR to practice their techniques and experience simulated competition environments. For sports like gymnastics and diving, however, the IOC offers only augmented reality (AR) visualization tools. The IOC claims full VR is only used where the complete athletic experience necessitates replication, <u>but Olympic sports are fundamentally about physical execution under pressure</u>, an aspect that is significantly diminished in AR-only visualization.

Which choice best describes the function of the underlined sentence in the text as a whole?

A) It identifies a feature of many Olympic sports that is not shared with the sports included in the AR visualization tools.

B) It presents a misconception about Olympic sports that the author believes is evident in the IOC's choice of training technologies.

C) It details a criticism of the IOC that the author defends against in the remainder of the sentence.

D) It presents a consideration that questions the IOC's rationale for using a technology with limited capabilities.

8

Recent studies of the Sahara Desert reveal surprising fluctuations in its size over the past century. Data collected from 1920 to 2020 show that the desert's boundaries have shifted by up to 800 kilometers. Typically, desert edges expand gradually due to increasing aridity. However, the Sahara's southern border has maintained an unusually stable position over decades, despite regional climate variations. The desert's average temperature rose steadily from 30°C to 35°C throughout the observation period, and its sand dunes showed unexpected stability. These findings challenge long-held assumptions about desertification processes. Some researchers propose that unseen climate events between 1900 and 1920 may have set the stage for this unusual behavior, potentially causing pre-stabilization of the border before the observation period began.

Based on the text, what does the data collected between 1920 and 2020 indicate about the southern border of the Sahara Desert?

A) It underwent several expansion and contraction cycles since researchers began studying it in 1920.

B) It was too arid to maintain the rate of sand dune movement typically seen in desert regions.

C) It had experienced significant climate changes before scientists began to observe it in 1920.

D) It had been inhibited from expanding as would happen normally in a desert environment.

9

Text 1
From about 250 CE to 900 CE, the Maya civilization flourished in Mesoamerica, particularly in the Yucatán Peninsula. Around 900 CE, the Maya mysteriously abandoned many of their great cities. Many researchers cite warfare and social unrest to explain why the Maya abandoned their urban centers. Citing defaced royal monuments, these researchers argue that increased conflict between city-states and internal social upheaval led to the collapse of the Maya civilization.

Text 2
Richard Hansen and colleagues conducted extensive archaeological excavations at several major Maya sites and uncovered evidence of extensive deforestation and soil erosion in the areas surrounding these cities. The team claims that the evidence is indisputable; environmental degradation led to agricultural collapse and resource depletion, ultimately driving the Maya to abandon their urban centers. They argue that the Maya's intensive agricultural practices and large-scale construction projects severely damaged the local ecosystem, making it increasingly difficult to sustain their growing population.

Based on the texts, how would Hansen and colleagues most likely respond to the many researchers in Text 1?

A) They would argue that the true answer remains inconclusive.

B) They would argue that their evidence confirms the researchers' claims in Text 1 about the Maya abandonment of their cities.

C) They would concede that it is one possible scenario but not the primary one.

D) They would question the researchers' claims in Text 1, citing evidence to the contrary.

10

In the United States, the preference for online shopping as a share of total retail sales increased by more than a third between 2010 and 2020. Such shifts are typically explained by appealing to the technology adoption model, which posits that consumer behavior is primarily influenced by perceived usefulness and ease of use of online shopping. However, a study by David Rodriguez on consumer behavior in multichannel retail environments (such as physical stores, online websites, mobile apps, or catalogues) shows how simplistic this model is. While perceived usefulness and ease of use did influence consumer choices, several other factors, such as the age of the consumer or income levels, significantly affected purchasing decisions across different retail channels.

Which of the following, if true, would best support Chen and Rodriguez's study?

A) Changes in consumer income levels significantly affect purchasing patterns in physical stores but not on online websites.

B) Perceived usefulness and ease of use are the sole determining factors in consumer channel choice across all countries and cultures.

C) The age of individuals strongly influences their likelihood of participating in online product reviews and ratings.

D) The level of education of consumers significantly impacts their engagement with different retail channels.

11

Average Annual Wage (in USD) for selected countries in 1990 and 2020

Country	1990	2020	Change in Wage	Percent Change
Canada	32,560	55,342	22,782	70%
Japan	30,600	40,861	10,261	34%
Germany	28,420	53,745	25,325	89%
Australia	27,850	54,401	26,551	95%

A student in a global economics course is analyzing the growth in average annual wages across different developed nations from 1990 to 2020. This analysis aims to understand the varying rates of wage growth and their potential impacts on global economic dynamics. The student's first task is to compare the wage growth in Japan to that of other countries. Based on the data, the student concludes that _____.

Which choice most effectively uses data from the table to complete the student's conclusion?

A) the percent increase in average annual wage was higher in Japan than in Canada, Germany, and Australia.

B) while the increase in average annual wage in Japan was less than that in Canada, Germany, and Australia, it still showed significant growth.

C) the average annual wage in Japan decreased between 1990 and 2020, unlike the growth seen in Canada, Germany, and Australia.

D) although the increase in average annual wage in Japan was greater than that in Canada, it was less than the increases seen in Germany and Australia.

12

One prevailing theory posits that the Permian-Triassic (P-T) extinction, Earth's most severe biotic crisis, was primarily caused by ocean acidification resulting from increased solar radiation. Recent research by Zhang and colleagues offers new insights. They analyzed mercury (Hg) isotopes in sedimentary rocks spanning the P-T boundary from multiple global sites, discovering a distinct negative mass-independent fractionation (MIF) of odd-mass Hg isotopes, consistent with Hg sourced from volcanic emissions. Additionally, the team identified elevated levels of methylmercury, a highly toxic compound destabilizing marine ecosystems known to form as a result of magmatic degassing. Coupled with existing evidence of rapid global warming during this period, the researchers posit that the P-T extinction event was most likely triggered by _____

Which choice most logically completes the text?

A) ocean acidification that intensified magmatic degassing, releasing large amounts of mercury into the environment.

B) prolonged volcanism that released both greenhouse gases and mercury, resulting in climatic destabilization and environmental toxicity.

C) intensification of solar radiation that accelerated the ocean acidification and the production of methylmercury.

D) a sudden release of mercury from deep-ocean sediments, leading to widespread toxicity in marine ecosystems.

13

Analysis of genetic material from various primate species has revealed insights into their evolutionary relationships and unique adaptations. A particular haplotype associated with basic cognitive functions was found in gorilla DNA, dating back to approximately 10 million years ago (MYA). A similar study of chimpanzee DNA identified this haplotype as emerging around 7 MYA in their lineage. In the early 2000s, researchers began identifying specific genes related to unique primate characteristics. One key discovery was the FOXP2 haplotype, linked to both language development and enhanced cognitive flexibility, which appeared in the primate lineage around 8 MYA. This fact helps explain why, whereas behaviors associated with advanced cognitive flexibility was found in _____

Which choice most logically completes the text?

A) both the chimpanzee and gorilla genome studies, only the latter included evidence of more complex vocal tract anatomy.

B) primate DNA sequenced before 2000, no such evidence was found in genomes analyzed later.

C) the gorilla genome study, no FOXP2 haplotype was found among the chimpanzee sequences analyzed.

D) the chimpanzee genome project, no such evidence was found in the gorilla genome study.

Test Score Growth in Three Different Device Policies

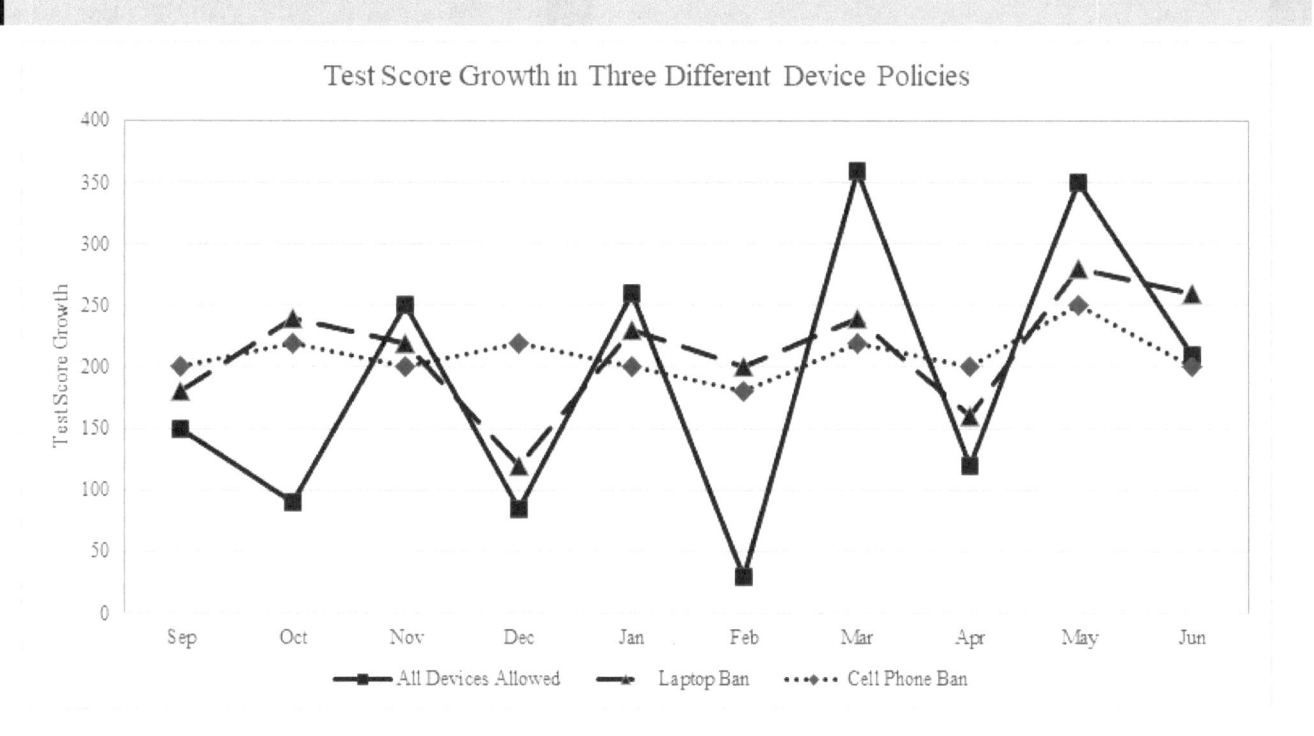

To investigate potential impact of electronic devices in academic performance, Dr. Phyllis Naver observed student academic performance across 75 high school classrooms with three different electronic device policies: cell phone bans only, laptops bans, and all devices allowed. Test scores in math and English were monitored monthly, allowing us to analyze trends and fluctuations over time. The study's extended duration provided insights into how different technology policies affect academic performance and stability over multiple academic years. Based on the data, Dr. Naver finds that _____.

Which choice most effectively uses data from the table to complete the statement?

A) students perform better academically during the beginning of the year than the end of the year.
B) the use of laptops in classrooms leads to higher test scores than the use of cell phones.
C) allowing all devices leads to the highest test scores.
D) the absence of cell phones helps to reduce variability in test score growth over time.

Edenbrook Test 4

15

Species	Total Examined	With Eyespots	Without Eyespots	Ratio (e:n)
M. peleides	120	108	12	9
C. memnon	85	82	3	27.33
B. anynana	200	176	24	7.33
H. erato	150	15	135	0.11
D. plexippus	180	36	144	0.25

Many butterflies have distinctive patterns on their wings, including eyespots, which are thought to play a role in predator deterrence. Dr. Sophia Chen, an entomologist at the University of Toronto, and her team conducted a study on various butterfly species to examine the prevalence of eyespots on their wings. They found that in some species, wings with eyespots are significantly more common than wings without eyespots, with ratios as high as _____.

Which choice most effectively uses data from the table to complete the text?

A) 27.33 to 1, as in the case of C. memnon.

B) 9.00 to 1, as in the case of M. peleides.

C) 0.11 to 1, as in the case of H. erato.

D) 180 to 36, as in the case of D. plexippus.

16

Carved, polished, and assembled from reclaimed wood, the furniture pieces of Barcelona-based Swedish designer Ingrid Johansson are designed to inspire users to reflect on their own connections to sustainable _____ her eco-conscious creations in the 2022 exhibition Natural Forms and Function at the Moderna Museet in Stockholm were equally compelling.

Which choice completes the text so that it conforms to the conventions of Standard English?

A) living and to

B) living and

C) living;

D) living

17

Characterized by their unique breathing apparatus, air-breathing vertebrates, such as the red-eyed tree frog (Agalychnis callidryas), _____ a complex and varied class of animals known as amphibians, a remarkable class of creatures capable of living both on land and in water.

Which choice completes the text so that it conforms to the conventions of Standard English?

A) comprise
B) comprises
C) has comprised
D) comprised

18

A pioneer in the field of quantum mechanics and recipient of the Nobel Prize in Physics, _____ revolutionized our understanding of atomic structure when he proposed his model of the atom with electrons orbiting the nucleus in fixed energy levels.

Which choice completes the text so that it conforms to the conventions of Standard English?

A) Danish physicist Niels Bohr's development of the quantum theory of the atom advanced the field of spectroscopy significantly
B) the development of the quantum theory of the atom by Danish physicist Niels Bohr led to significant advancements in the field of spectroscopy
C) spectroscopy saw significant advancements due to Danish physicist Niels Bohr who developed the quantum theory of the atom
D) Danish physicist Niels Bohr developed the quantum theory of the atom and made significant advancements in the field of spectroscopy

19

The Nobel Prize is renowned worldwide as a prestigious award for outstanding achievements in various fields. However, few know that the prize originated from a misunderstanding in 1888, when Alfred Nobel's brother Ludvig died and a French newspaper erroneously published Alfred's obituary instead. Shocked by being remembered as a "merchant of death" due to his invention of dynamite, Nobel decided to leave a better legacy by establishing prizes to honor those who _____ humanity in physics, chemistry, medicine, literature, and peace.

Which choice completes the text so that it conforms to the conventions of Standard English?

A) benefit:
B) benefit
C) benefit,
D) benefit;

20

French culinary expert Hervé This is celebrated for his groundbreaking _____ so innovative that they've revolutionized cooking techniques, This's molecular gastronomy experiments blend science and cuisine in ways previously unimaginable.

Which choice completes the text so that it conforms to the conventions of Standard English?

A) research, findings
B) research. Findings
C) research and findings
D) research: findings

21

Many people dream of visiting the pristine beaches of the Maldives. The rising sea levels caused by climate change are threatening these tropical _____ the islands' average height is only about five feet above sea level.

Which choice completes the text so that it conforms to the conventions of Standard English?

A) paradise. Unfortunately,
B) paradise, unfortunately;
C) paradise; unfortunately,
D) paradise, unfortunately,

22

Since its inception in 1869, *Nature* has been a leading scientific journal, publishing groundbreaking research across various disciplines. In 2020, the journal introduced new guidelines for authors submitting research papers, a decision made to uphold such _____ reproducibility, rigor, and transparency in scientific reporting.

Which choice completes the text so that it conforms to the conventions of Standard English?

A) standards as the journals,
B) standards: as the journals,
C) standards, as the journal's
D) standards as the journal's

23

Biologists agree that the naturalist Charles Darwin was not the first to propose the idea of evolution. No one can deny, _____ that Darwin's groundbreaking theory of natural selection and extensive field research revolutionized biology as a discipline during the 19th century.

Which choice completes the text so that it conforms to the conventions of Standard English?

A) as a result,
B) in other words,
C) though,
D) in addition,

24

The Renaissance period saw a surge in artistic and scientific achievements throughout Europe. Many great thinkers and artists emerged during this time, revolutionizing fields like painting, sculpture, and astronomy. _____ the Renaissance sparked a renewed interest in classical learning, leading to advancements in literature, philosophy, and education.

Which choice completes the text with the most logical transition?

A) Subsequently,
B) In contrast,
C) In fact,
D) Furthermore,

25

While researching a topic, a student has taken the following notes:

- The Pulitzer Prize for Fiction has been awarded annually since 1948, recognizing distinguished fiction by American authors.
- Junot Díaz and Viet Thanh Nguyen are authors from immigrant backgrounds who have won the Pulitzer Prize for Fiction.
- Junot Díaz was born in the Dominican Republic and immigrated to the United States as a child.
- Junot Diaz won a Pulitzer Prize for *The Brief Wondrous Life of Oscar Wao* in 2008.
- Viet Thanh Nguyen was born in Vietnam and came to the United States as a refugee with his family in 1975.
- Viet Thanh Nguyen won a Pulitzer Prize for *The Sympathizer* in 2016.

The student wants to specify the different backgrounds of the two prize-winning authors. Which choice most effectively uses relevant information from the notes to accomplish this goal?

A) *The Brief Wondrous Life of Oscar Wao* and *The Sympathizer* are both Pulitzer Prize-winning novels, but the former is by Junot Díaz, whereas the latter is by Viet Thanh Nguyen.

B) Junot Díaz, of Dominican descent, won the Pulitzer in 2008, whereas Viet Thanh Nguyen, of Vietnamese descent, received this prestigious award in 2016.

C) Junot Díaz and Viet Thanh Nguyen are both Pulitzer Prize-winning authors from immigrant backgrounds.

D) *The Brief Wondrous Life of Oscar Wao* and *The Sympathizer* are both novels by authors from immigrant backgrounds that have won the Pulitzer Prize for Fiction.

26

While researching a topic, a student has taken the following notes:

- The Reproducibility Index (RI) is a ten-point scale that assesses the replicability of scientific experiments.
- Experiments with higher RI scores are considered more replicable than those with lower scores.
- Experiments with an RI of 1-5 are considered poorly replicable, while those with an RI of 6-10 are considered highly replicable.
- A study on cognitive biases has an RI of 2.
- A study on memory formation has an RI of 6.
- A study on decision-making processes has an RI of 9.

The student wants to compare the replicability of the cognitive biases study and the memory formation study. Which choice most effectively uses relevant information from the notes to accomplish this goal?

A) The study on cognitive biases is poorly replicable, while the study on memory formation and the study on decision-making processes are highly replicable.

B) The study on memory formation is highly replicable, while the study on cognitive biases is not replicable.

C) The study on decision-making processes is more replicable than the study on cognitive biases based on their respective RI scores.

D) The study on memory formation is considered highly replicable, while the study on cognitive biases falls in the poorly replicable range.

27

While researching a topic, a student has taken the following notes:

- Coffee is a popular beverage consumed worldwide, known for its stimulating effects due to caffeine content.
- There are two main commercially cultivated coffee species: Arabica and Robusta.
- Arabica beans are generally considered to have a superior flavor but are more expensive to produce.
- Robusta beans have a stronger taste and higher caffeine content but are less expensive.
- Many commercial coffee blends use a combination of both Arabica and Robusta beans.

The student wants to make a generalization about the types of coffee beans used in commercial coffee production. Which choice most effectively uses relevant information from the notes to accomplish this goal?

A) While different beans are used in commercial coffee production, they are often blended to balance quality and cost.

B) Arabica beans are generally considered to have a superior flavor but are more expensive to produce than Robusta beans.

C) Coffee's worldwide popularity is due to its stimulating effects, which come from its caffeine content.

D) Robusta beans have a stronger taste and higher caffeine content compared to Arabica beans.

STOP

Reading and Writing

32 MINUTES, 27 QUESTIONS

DIRECTIONS

The questions in this section address a number of important reading and writing skills. Each question includes one or more passages, which may include a table or graph. Read each passage and question carefully, and then choose the best answer to the question based on the passage(s).

All questions in this section are multiple-choice with four answer choices. Each question has a single best answer.

1

The Impressionist movement revolutionized the art world in the late 19th century with its innovative techniques and subjects. Led by artists like Claude Monet and Pierre-Auguste Renoir, this style _____ the academic traditions of the Salon by focusing on capturing the fleeting effects of light and atmosphere in everyday scenes to achieve a more spontaneous and vibrant representation of the world.

Which choice completes the text with the most logical and precise word or phrase?

A) invented
B) misinterpreted
C) rejected
D) recanted

2

Recent analysis by marine biologists Dr. Amelia Thornton and Dr. Rajesh Patel highlights an intriguing disparity in oceanic research: while studies on the behavioral patterns of surface-dwelling fish species are _____, the complex social structures of deep-sea organisms inhabiting hydrothermal vent ecosystems, such as the Pompeii worm and yeti crab, have attracted notably less scientific attention.

Which choice completes the text with the most logical and precise word or phrase?

A) sporadic
B) tentative
C) copious
D) ambivalent

3

Scientists like Marie Curie contributed to the expansion of physics research in the years following the discovery of radioactivity, which occurred in 1896. Laboratories from this era represent _____ portion of what is considered the foundation of modern nuclear physics, but eighteenth-century experimenters like Benjamin Franklin should be considered just as crucial to the physics research timeline.

Which choice completes the text with the most logical and precise word or phrase?

A) a volatile

B) a tenacious

C) an outsized

D) an infinitismal

4

The following excerpt is from a 19th-century novel. The narrator and his companion has finally reached the premises of his new employment.

> As we approached the grand manor, its imposing facade loomed before us, the windows dark and forbidding. My companion, ever the contrarian, muttered his misgivings about our visit, his words sharp and cutting in the stillness. At the very gates, we found our progress checked by an overgrown hedge, which argued every inch of our advance with its thorny tendrils. The carriage wheels groaned in protest, echoing my companion's earlier remonstrations, as we pushed forward through the verdant obstruction.

As used in the passage, what does the word "argued" most nearly mean?

A) Debated with

B) Complained about

C) Reasoned against

D) Prevented access to

5

A recent set studies of Arctic climate change has revealed a complex chain reaction of environmental shifts. In a 2023 study on Arctic climate change, Dr. Sarah Chen's team analyzed methane concentrations, revealing a 15% increase since 2010 and a corresponding 0.4°C temperature rise. At the same time, Dr. Mark Rodriguez's oceanographic research found that the warming Arctic Ocean has accelerated polar jet stream fluctuations by 22%, intensifying extreme weather events in North America. Building on these findings, Dr. Emily Nkosi's ecological survey documented a 30% decline in polar bear populations, while observing unexpected behaviors in Arctic foxes.

Which choice best describes the overall structure of the text?

A) It details atmospheric methane increases and temperature changes, explores ocean-driven weather pattern shifts, and identifies an unexpected cause for these changes.

B) It analyzes Arctic methane increases and corresponding temperatures, explains the consequence of jet streams on ocean warming, and documents the impact on two species.

C) It finds a correlation between atmospheric gas and temperature, explores the impacts of warming in the Arctic Ocean, and examines wildlife trends and adaptations.

D) It introduces notable trends in the Arctic Ocean, analyzes the results of alterations in the marine current, and compares conservation efforts for two Arctic species.

6

The implementation of carbon capture and storage (CCS) technology in coal-fired power plants has been heralded by some as a crucial step towards mitigating climate change. Proponents argue that CCS could reduce CO_2 emissions by up to 90% while allowing continued use of abundant coal resources. However, environmental scientists caution that the long-term viability of underground CO_2 storage remains unproven, and the energy-intensive nature of the capture process may offset a significant portion of the emissions savings. Moreover, economic analysts point out that the high capital costs of retrofitting existing plants with CCS technology could make coal-based electricity less competitive compared to renewable alternatives.

According to the text, why do some experts express reservations about the widespread adoption of (CCS) ?

A) The technology is not sufficiently advanced to capture a meaningful amount of CO_2 emissions.

B) There are concerns about the safety of transporting captured CO_2 to storage sites.

C) The technology's sustained effectiveness of CO_2 storage and net environmental benefit are subject to debate

D) The high capital expenditure for implementing CCS technology can be offset by its long-term economic viability.

7

The Heisenberg Uncertainty Principle, fundamental to quantum mechanics, states that precisely measuring certain paired quantities simultaneously is impossible. This isn't due to instrumental limitations, but a core property of quantum systems. Intriguingly, this principle has parallels in information theory, manifesting as a trade-off between message length and transmission accuracy. In communication systems, maximizing data throughput often increases error rates, mirroring quantum mechanical constraints.

What does the passage suggest about the relationship between quantum mechanics and information theory?

A) Quantum systems manifest limitations in precision while information theory exhibits limitations in completeness.

B) Information theory overcomes constraints that remain fixed in quantum systems, primarily in message length and transmission accuracy.

C) Information theory and quantum systems were developed as an application of a fundamental principle.

D) Both quantum systems and information theory exhibit similar constraints on two shared and fundamental aspects.

8

Recent marine biology studies have revealed complex interactions in coral reef ecosystems. Dr. Tanaka's research on the Great Barrier Reef demonstrated that coral health directly influences both predator and prey populations, often overriding traditional predator-prey dynamics. Similarly, Dr. Chen's work in the Caribbean found that seasonal water temperature fluctuations were the primary driver of species distribution patterns, with predation pressure playing a secondary role. These findings highlight the intricate web of factors shaping marine ecosystems beyond simple predator-prey relationships.

Based on the text, the author would most likely agree with which statement about the factors that shape coral reef ecosystems?

A) The seasonal water temperature fluctuations shape complex interactions between coral reef systems and predator and prey.

B) The overall health and condition of the coral reef structure itself plays a more significant role than seasonal water temperature variations.

C) The complex interplay between water temperature fluctuations and predation pressure create species distribution patterns.

D) The combined influence of coral health and seasonal temperature variations affect the distributions of predator and prey populations.

9

In a study on brand perception and consumer behavior, researchers led by Dr. Amelia Chen examined the relationship between brand loyalty and product diversification strategies. They compared firms that used related diversification (leveraging existing core competencies to enter similar markets, such as a smartphone manufacturer expanding into tablets) with those that employed unrelated diversification (entering completely different industries, like a soft drink company acquiring a movie studio). The researchers concluded that related diversification generally leads to higher brand loyalty compared to unrelated diversification.

Which of the following findings, if true, would most strongly support Dr. Chen's conclusion?

A) A leading athletic shoe company's expansion into digital cameras resulted in a 20% increase in brand loyalty, while their expansion into athletic apparel only led to a 10% increase.

B) A leading shipping company's launch of a package tracking app resulted in a 25% boost in brand loyalty, whereas their entry into bulk freight services only led to a 22% increase.

C) A popular soft drink company's acquisition of a snack food brand led to a 30% increase in brand loyalty, while their acquisition of a bottled water company resulted in only a 20% increase.

D) A meal kit company's introduction of online cooking classes was adopted by 78% of its existing customers, whereas its expansion into a line of casual clothing only attracted 15%.

10

Measure	Mean PBL Scores	Mean TL Scores
Critical thinking	7.8	6.5
Problem-solving	8.2	7.1
Creativity	6.9	7.7

To evaluate the effectiveness of different teaching methods, researchers compared outcomes for students taught using Problem-Based Learning (PBL) and Traditional Lecture (TL) methods. PBL emphasizes collaborative problem-solving and self-directed learning, while TL relies on instructor-led presentations. After a semester, students were assessed on various skills. The results show mean scores for each group across different measures. Researchers concluded that PBL is superior to TL because _____.

Which choice most effectively uses data from the table to complete the assertion?

A) it resulted in higher critical thinking and problem-solving scores, despite lower creativity scores

B) it showed consistently higher scores across all measured skills.

C) it demonstrated higher creativity, despite lower critical thinking scores.

D) its highest score was in problem solving while the lowest score was in creativity.

11

Dr. Amelia Selim and her colleagues investigated the behavior and function of neutrophils, a type of white blood cell, during various infections. They found that during simulated bacterial infections in vitro, 78% of neutrophils exhibited rapid chemotaxis and phagocytosis within 30 minutes. The response ranged from increased motility in *Staphylococcus aureus* infections to enhanced degranulation in *Escherichia coli* infections. Although neutrophils are known to respond to various pathogens, the researchers claim that neutrophils play a more critical role in the early stages of bacterial infections compared to viral infections.

Which finding, if true, would most directly support Dr. Selim and colleagues' claim?

A) In mouse models, depletion of neutrophils led to a significant increase in bacterial load within 6 hours of infection, while viral titers were not significantly affected until 24 hours post-infection.

B) In viral infections, neutrophils showed peak activity during the initial symptoms, while for bacterial infections, peak neutrophil infiltration was observed after the onset of severe symptoms.

C) In most cases, the neutrophils exhibited chemotaxis and phagocytosis when encountering both bacterial and viral pathogens.

D) Neutrophil extracellular traps (NETs) were deployed at concentrations detectable by most bacterial species, but not at levels that could effectively trap viral particles.

12

Hamlet is a 17th-century play by William Shakespeare. In the play, Hamlet expresses the idea that the fear of the unknown after death prevents people from ending their lives, claiming _____

Which quotation from *Hamlet* most effectively illustrates the claim?

A) "To be, or not to be, that is the question:"

B) "To die, to sleep— / No more—and by a sleep to say we end / The heartache and the thousand natural shocks / That flesh is heir to"

C) "But that the dread of something after death, / The undiscovered country from whose bourn / No traveler returns, puzzles the will"

D) "Thus conscience does make cowards of us all, / And thus the native hue of resolution / Is sicklied o'er with the pale cast of thought"

13

The International Language Acquisition Project (ILAP) studies language development in children across 30 countries from birth to age 18. Like most comprehensive longitudinal studies, ILAP requires a large team of researchers and generates vast amounts of data due to its long-term nature and broad scope. In contrast, a single-site vocabulary assessment on vocabulary growth in preschoolers over a six-month period is relatively straightforward. This type of focused, short-term research may not face the same logistical challenges because _____.

Which choice most logically completes the text?

A) 30 countries provide enough diversity for ILAP to draw meaningful conclusions.

B) longitudinal studies always yield more reliable results than short-term research.

C) preschoolers typically have a more limited vocabulary range compared to older children.

D) a single-site vocabulary assessment can be conducted without complex coordination.

14

Particle collisions in the Large Hadron Collider (LHC) have been reaching higher energies in response to accelerator upgrades, potentially enabling increased detection of rare Higgs boson decay events through greater luminosity and collision frequency, but also potentially inhibiting detection due to the increased background noise through greater production of secondary particles. Physicist Maria Chen and her colleagues developed a model incorporating numerous inputs—years of collision data and detector efficiency metrics among them—to evaluate the effects of higher-energy collisions on the signal-to-noise ratio in Higgs boson detection, concluding that higher energy can lead to increased boson detection.

Which finding, if true, would most directly weaken the researchers' conclusion?

A) Higher collision energies amplify the effect of beam luminosity and collision frequency on both the production of Higgs bosons and the rate of background particle generation.

B) Higher collision energies suppress luminosity and subdue collision frequency, but they raise the rate of background particle production.

C) Higher collision energies deplete the production of beam luminosity and collision frequency, and they suppress background particle generation.

D) Higher collision energies heighten luminosity and accelerate collision frequency but have no effect on the rate of background particle production.

15

Prolonged exposure to oxidative stress can affect cellular organelles, as Maria Chen and David Lee found in a 2018 study of mitochondria in fibroblasts. Researchers conducted a meta-analysis of studies on how oxidative stress affects various cellular components and found that, for every study, relevant structural or functional parameters of the organelles were observably different between the stressed group and the otherwise similar but unstressed group. Although, on average, studies of mitochondria showed larger differences than studies of endoplasmic reticulum did, for every organelle examined, there were individual studies showing differences well above the average for mitochondria. Therefore, the results of the meta-analysis suggest that _____

Which choice most logically completes the text?

A) the difference found in the study conducted by Maria Chen and David Lee was likely larger than the average difference for studies of mitochondria in fibroblasts included in the meta-analysis.

B) the studies in the meta-analysis that examined mitochondria were more likely than those that examined endoplasmic reticulum to specify whether the observed effects were reversible.

C) the differences that studies attribute to exposure to oxidative stress are likely to be more pronounced for endoplasmic reticulum than they are for mitochondria.

D) some studies of endoplasmic reticulum found larger effects of exposure to oxidative stress than some studies of mitochondria did.

16

Featured in Echoes of the Past, a 2022 collective showcase at the Metropolitan Museum of Art in New York City, was the creation of sculptor Maya Lin, who is renowned for her large-scale environmental installations that blend natural landscapes with geometric forms. Her art explores themes of ecology, sustainability, and _____ she is recognized for revolutionizing the field of site-specific sculpture.

Which choice completes the text so that it conforms to the conventions of Standard English?

A) cultural identity, and
B) cultural identity,
C) cultural identity:
D) cultural identity and

17

Astronomers estimate our Milky Way galaxy to be approximately 100,000 light-years in diameter, containing over 500 billion stars. Using advanced telescopes, _____

Which choice completes the text so that it conforms to the conventions of Standard English?

A) astrophysicist Dr. Sarah Johnson's study places our galaxy in the "medium-large" category of known galaxies.

B) a study by astrophysicist Dr. Sarah Johnson places our galaxy in the "medium-large" category of known galaxies

C) astrophysicist Dr. Sarah Johnson places our galaxy in the "medium-large" category of known galaxies.

D) our galaxy places in the "medium-large" category of known galaxies, according to astrophysicist Dr. Sarah Johnson.

18

In 1995, computer scientist Fei-Fei Li developed an innovative approach in machine learning that enabled her to analyze and categorize large-scale visual datasets. A decade later, she _____ for this pioneering work with the J.K. Aggarwal Prize in Computer Vision and the Longuet-Higgins Prize at the Conference on Computer Vision and Pattern Recognition and regarded as the pioneer of deep learning in artificial intelligence.

Which choice completes the text so that it conforms to the conventions of Standard English?

A) is recognized
B) had been recognized
C) recognized
D) would be recognized

19

The Montessori method is an approach to education _____ to nurture learning in the same natural way children explore their environment, prioritizes hands-on experiences and self-directed activity from a very young age. In Montessori classrooms, students begin their educational journey with simple practical life exercises like pouring water or buttoning clothes.

Which choice completes the text so that it conforms to the conventions of Standard English?

A) that seeks
B) that has sought
C) that, seeking
D) that is seeking

20

Dog breeds can be categorized by how much exercise they require daily. For example, high-energy breeds like Border Collies need extensive exercise, placing them in the high-maintenance _____ only moderate activity, Bulldogs are instead considered low-maintenance.

Which choice completes the text so that it conforms to the conventions of Standard English?

A) group, requiring
B) group and require
C) group. Requiring
D) group and requiring

21

Housed in a stunning neoclassical building, the National Gallery's extensive assortment of marble sculptures and bronze statues, which includes Michelangelo's *David* and Bernini's *Apollo and Daphne*, _____ among its most awe-inspiring attractions.

Which choice completes the text so that it conforms to the conventions of Standard English?

A) stands
B) stand
C) have stood
D) were standing

22

According to the Sapir-Whorf hypothesis, languages with polysynthetic morphology tend to shape their speakers' worldviews, wherein intricate lexical-grammatical patterns significantly influence perception and cognition. _____ languages with analytic morphology tend to foster more cognitively flexible thinking, under which speakers can more easily adapt to diverse cultural paradigms.

Which choice completes the text with the most logical transition?

A) Consequently,
B) In fact,
C) Conversely,
D) That is,

23

The old lighthouse stood atop a rocky cliff, its beacon warning ships of the dangerous shoreline. _____ amid the crashing waves and salty air, generations of keepers had maintained their lonely vigil.

Which choice completes the text with the most logical transition?

A) Hence,
B) Fittingly,
C) In fact,
D) There,

24

The development of the polio vaccine in the 1950s was a major breakthrough in the fight against this devastating disease, which primarily affected children and could cause paralysis or even death. _____ the success of the vaccine was not immediate, as it took years of widespread immunization campaigns and public health efforts to effectively control and eventually eliminate polio in many parts of the world.

Which choice completes the text with the most logical transition?

A) That being said,

B) Accordingly,

C) Indeed,

D) As a result,

25

The Amazon rainforest is often called the "lungs of the Earth" due to its vast capacity to absorb carbon dioxide and produce oxygen. _____ this process of photosynthesis not only cleans the air but also helps regulate global climate patterns by influencing rainfall and temperature across continents.

Which choice completes the text with the most logical transition?

A) In reality,

B) In fact,

C) In turn,

D) In addition,

26

While researching a topic, a student has taken the following notes:

- Wilhelm Ostwald was a German chemist and philosopher.
- He is known for his work in physical chemistry and catalysis.
- Ostwald developed the Ostwald process for producing nitric acid.
- The process was first patented on October 17, 1902.
- It was initially implemented at a factory in Gerthe, Germany.

The student wants to emphasize emphasize when and where the Ostwald process was first implemented. Which choice most effectively uses relevant information from the notes to accomplish this goal?

A) Wilhelm Ostwald, a German chemist, made significant contributions to physical chemistry and catalysis throughout his career.

B) The Ostwald process, patented in 1902, revolutionized the production of nitric acid in the early 20th century.

C) In 1902, Wilhelm Ostwald's innovative method for producing nitric acid was first put into practice at a factory in Gerthe, Germany.

D) The Ostwald process, developed by the renowned German chemist Wilhelm Ostwald, is an important industrial method for producing nitric acid.

27

While researching a topic, a student has taken the following notes:

- The Great Barrier Reef is the world's largest coral reef system.
- It is located off the coast of Queensland in northeastern Australia.
- The reef covers an area of approximately 344,400 square kilometers.
- It was formed about 20 million years ago.
- The reef is home to over 1,500 species of fish.
- Climate change is causing coral bleaching, threatening the reef's ecosystem.

The student wants to specify the size and location of the Great Barrier Reef. Which choice most effectively uses relevant information from the notes to accomplish this goal?

A) The Great Barrier Reef covers approximately 344,400 square kilometers off the coast of Queensland in northeastern Australia.

B) The Great Barrier Reef covers approximately 344,400 square kilometers and is home to over 1,500 species of fish.

C) Located off the coast of Queensland in northeastern Australia, the Great Barrier Reef was formed about 20 million years ago.

D) The Great Barrier Reef is threatened by climate change and coral bleaching, affecting its 1,500 species of fish.

STOP

TEST 4 ANSWER KEY

MODULE 1			MODULE 2		
1. A	10. D	19. B	1. C	10. A	19. C
2. A	11. B	20. B	2. C	11. A	20. C
3. D	12. B	21. B	3. C	12. C	21. A
4. B	13. D	22. D	4. D	13. D	22. C
5. D	14. D	23. C	5. C	14. B	23. D
6. A	15. A	24. D	6. C	15. D	24. A
7. D	16. C	25. B	7. D	16. A	25. B
8. D	17. A	26. D	8. D	17. C	26. C
9. D	18. D	27. A	9. D	18. D	27. A

To calculate your score, tally up the total number of correct answers from both Module 1 and Module 2. This is your RAW SCORE. Find your raw score below and your scaled score range is on the right.

Module 1 _____ + Module 2 _____ = Total Raw _____ = SCORE RANGE _____

TEST 3 – RAW SCORE CONVERSION

RAW SCORE (TOTAL CORRECT)	SCORE RANGE	RAW SCORE (TOTAL CORRECT)	SCORE RANGE
54	800-800	27	450-500
53	790-800	26	440-500
52	780-800	25	430-490
51	770-790	24	420-480
50	750-780	23	410-470
49	730-770	22	400-460
48	720-760	21	390-450
47	710-750	20	380-440
46	700-740	19	370-430
45	690-730	18	360-420
44	670-710	17	350-410
43	650-700	16	340-400
42	630-680	15	330-390
41	610-660	14	320-380
40	590-640	13	310-370
39	570-620	12	300-360
38	560-610	11	290-350
37	550-600	10	280-340
36	540-590	9	270-330
35	530-580	8	260-320
34	520-570	7	250-310
33	510-560	6	240-300
32	500-550	5	230-290
31	490-540	4	220-280
30	480-530	3	210-270
29	470-520	2	200-260
28	460-510	1	200-250

TEST 4: MODULE 1 ANSWER EXPLANATIONS

1. **Answer: A. Sentence completion.** The clues are *persistent efforts* and *shaping public opinion...* These phrases suggest that the scientists are fighting for, or advocating for, stricter regulations. Eliminate B; **rationalizing** means to explain away or justify, even if untrue. Eliminate C; **deliberating** means considering carefully. Eliminate D; **impeding** means to block or obstruct.

2. **Answer: A. Sentence completion.** The clues are *endless ice fields...but in reality* and *rich tapestry of diverse*. Taken together, the Arctic should be diverse, or *far from* **homogeneous**, which means uniform. Eliminate B; **interdependent** means dependent on each other. Eliminate C; **prolific** means producing a lot. Eliminate D; **trendy** means fashionable.

3. **Answer: D. Sentence completion.** The clues are *small residential projects* and *self-taught professional early in his career*. These phrases suggest that Tadao Ando's designs are present, or **featured**, in prestigious buildings around the world, while his earlier work was mainly focused on smaller projects in Osaka. Eliminate A; **contained** means to be confined within certain limits. Eliminate B; **invented** means to create something that did not exist before. Eliminate C; **adjusted** means to adapt or modify something to fit a specific purpose.

4. **Answer: B. Vocab in context.** The clues are *beset by every conceivable hardship* and the vivid descriptions that follow, such as *rains fell with a ferocity heretofore unknown, earth beneath our feet into a quagmire of despair*, and *Beasts of terrifying aspect lurked in the shadows*. These phrases suggest that the expedition encountered all **possible,** or imaginable, hardships. Eliminate A; **Noticeable** means easily seen or detected, which doesn't capture the comprehensive nature of the hardships described. Eliminate **C) Fanciful**; fanciful means imaginative or whimsical, which contradicts the serious tone of the passage. Eliminate **D) Believable**; believable means capable of being believed, which is close in meaning but doesn't fully capture the idea of encompassing all possibilities.

5. **Answer: D. Sentence completion.** The clues are *replacing rationalist and empiricist traditions* and *profoundly shaping subsequent philosophical discourse*. These phrases suggest that Kant's works went beyond and replaced previous philosophical traditions while significantly influencing future philosophy. Eliminate A; **echoed** means to repeat or imitate. Eliminate B; **detained** means to hold back or restrain. Eliminate C; **supplemented** means to add to or enhance. "**Superseded**" correctly conveys that Kant's works replaced and went beyond the works of other Enlightenment thinkers, aligning with the description of his philosophical impact and influence on modern Western philosophy.

6. **Answer: A. Function.** Use process of elimination. Eliminate Choice B; the passage doesn't mention any limitations in the data. Eliminate Choice C; while the text mentions implications for searching for extraterrestrial life, it doesn't explicitly suggest future research avenues. Eliminate Choice D; the last sentence doesn't call into question the assumptions guiding the research, but rather challenges pre-existing assumptions about life. The last sentence states that the discovery *has expanded our understanding of the diverse conditions under which life can flourish, challenging long-held*

assumptions about the necessity of sunlight for sustaining life on Earth and beyond. This **elaborates on the implications of the study's primary findings** by showing how the discovery of chemosynthetic ecosystems has broadened our understanding of life's potential habitats and challenged previous assumptions.

7. **Answer: D. Function.** Use process of elimination. Eliminate Choice A; the sentence doesn't identify a feature unique to certain Olympic sports, but rather a characteristic common to all Olympic sports. Eliminate Choice B; the sentence doesn't present a misconception, but rather a factual statement about the nature of Olympic sports. Eliminate Choice C; the sentence doesn't detail a criticism that the author defends against, but rather presents a point that challenges the IOC's rationale. The underlined sentence states that *Olympic sports are fundamentally about physical execution under pressure*, which contrasts with the IOC's claim about when to use full VR. This **questions the IOC's rationale** for using AR visualization tools, which have *limited capabilities* in replicating the full athletic experience, including the pressure of competition.

8. **Answer: D. Detail.** Use process of elimination. Eliminate Choice A; the passage mentions fluctuations in the Sahara Desert's size, not its southern border. Eliminate Choice B; while the text mentions sand dune stability, it doesn't attribute this to excessive aridity. Eliminate Choice C; while the passage suggests pre-1920 events may have influenced the border, this is not indicated by the 1920-2020 data. The passage states that *the Sahara's southern border has maintained an unusually stable position over decades, despite regional climate variations*. This **had been inhibited from expanding** as would normally happen in a desert environment, which is further supported by the statement that *these findings challenge long-held assumptions about desertification processes*.

9. **Answer: D. Cross-text.** First identify the argument of the **many researchers** in Text 1: *Citing defaced royal monuments, these researchers argue that increased conflict between city-states and internal social upheaval led to the collapse of the Maya civilization*. Notice here that *these researchers* refers to *Many researchers* who *cite warfare and social unrest to explain why the Maya abandoned their urban centers*. Now, identify the line that discusses this in Text 2. You can connect *collapse of the Maya civilization* in Text 1 to *abandon their urban centers* in Text 2: *The team claims that the evidence is indisputable; environmental degradation led to agricultural collapse and resource depletion, ultimately driving the Maya to abandon their urban centers*. Notice here that the answer is *They would question the researchers' claims in Text 1, citing evidence to the contrary*. Eliminate Choice A; Hansen and colleagues claim their evidence is "indisputable," so they wouldn't argue the answer remains inconclusive. Eliminate Choice B; Hansen and colleagues present a different explanation (environmental factors) than the researchers in Text 1 (warfare and social unrest), so they wouldn't confirm Text 1's claims. Eliminate Choice C; The phrase "the evidence is indisputable" in Text 2 indicates that Hansen and colleagues would not consider warfare and social unrest as a possible primary scenario, but rather would **question the researchers' claims in Text 1, citing evidence to the contrary**.

10. **Answer: D. Supporting claims.** Identify the claim to support: *While perceived usefulness and ease of use did influence consumer choices, several other factors, such as the age of the consumer or income levels, significantly affected purchasing decisions across different retail channels.* Eliminate

Choice A; it contradicts the study's findings by suggesting income levels only affect physical store purchases, not online ones. Eliminate Choice B; it directly contradicts the study's claim by stating that perceived usefulness and ease of use are the *sole* determining factors. Eliminate Choice C; while it mentions age as a factor, it only relates to online reviews and ratings, not purchasing decisions across different retail channels. Choice D best supports the claim; link **level of education** = *several other factors*, **significantly impacts their engagement with different retail channels** = *significantly affected purchasing decisions across different retail channels*. Education level is another demographic factor similar to age and income, which the study suggests influence consumer behavior across channels.

11. **Answer: B. Infographics and detail.** First, identify the nature of the task: The student is comparing wage growth in Japan to that of other countries from 1990 to 2020. Next, evaluate each choice based on accuracy and relevance to the data provided:

    A) Inaccurate: The percent increase for Japan (34%) is lower than all other countries shown (Canada 70%, Germany 89%, Australia 95%).
    B) Accurate and relevant: Japan's increase (34%) is indeed less than Canada (70%), Germany (89%), and Australia (95%), but still shows growth from 30,690 to 40,891.
    C) Inaccurate: The data shows Japan's average annual wage increased from 30,690 to 40,891, not decreased.
    D) Inaccurate: While Japan's increase (10,201) was greater than Canada's (22,782), it was less than both Germany's (25,325) and Australia's (26,551).

    Choice B best supports the student's conclusion as it accurately reflects the data showing Japan's wage growth was positive but lower than the other countries listed.

12. **Answer B. Logical completion.** Identify the line of reasoning: 1) The P-T extinction was previously thought to be caused by ocean acidification from increased solar radiation. 2) New research found evidence of volcanic mercury emissions and elevated methylmercury levels. 3) There's existing evidence of rapid global warming during this period. Eliminate Choice A; it reverses the cause-effect relationship, suggesting ocean acidification caused magmatic degassing. Eliminate Choice C; it maintains the original theory of solar radiation, which the new evidence doesn't support. Eliminate Choice D; while it mentions mercury, it contradicts the evidence of volcanic origins. Choice B is consistent with the new evidence, linking prolonged volcanism to both the release of greenhouse gases (explaining global warming) and mercury (explaining the isotope findings and methylmercury levels), thus logically completing the text.

13. **Answer: D. Logical completion.** Identify the line of reasoning: 1) A cognitive function-related haplotype was found in gorilla DNA from 10 MYA and in chimpanzee DNA from 7 MYA. 2) The FOXP2 haplotype, linked to language and cognitive flexibility, appeared in primates around 8 MYA. 3) The question implies a difference in cognitive flexibility between species. Eliminate Choice A; it introduces new information about vocal tract anatomy not mentioned in the passage. Eliminate Choice B; it contradicts the timeline, as the FOXP2 discovery was made in the early 2000s. Eliminate Choice C; it contradicts the information that chimpanzees have the cognitive function haplotype.

Choice D logically completes the text because the chimpanzee lineage (7 MYA) aligns more closely with the FOXP2 emergence (8 MYA) than the gorilla lineage (10 MYA), suggesting advanced cognitive flexibility would be found in chimpanzee genomes but not in gorilla genomes.

14. **Answer: D. Infographics & detail.** First, identify the aim of the study: Dr. Naver's study investigates *how different electronic device policies affect academic performance and stability over time*. Next, evaluate each choice based on accuracy and relevance to the data provided:

    A) Inaccurate: The graph doesn't show a consistent pattern of better performance at the beginning of the year across all policies.
    B) Inaccurate: While laptops often show higher scores than cell phones, this isn't consistent throughout the year, and "All Devices Allowed" frequently outperforms both.
    C) Partially accurate but inconsistent: "All Devices Allowed" does show the highest peaks, but also the lowest valleys, indicating high variability rather than consistently highest scores.
    D) Accurate and relevant: The "Cell Phone Ban" line (dotted) shows the most stable trend with the least fluctuation over time, while "All Devices Allowed" (solid black) shows the highest variability. This supports the conclusion that absence of cell phones reduces variability in test score growth over time.

15. **Answer: A. Infographics & logical complete.** Identify the line of reasoning: 1) The study examines the prevalence of eyespots on butterfly wings. 2) In some species, wings with eyespots are significantly more common. 3) The text asks for the highest ratio of wings with eyespots to those without. Next, evaluate each choice based on accuracy and relevance to the data provided:

    A) Accurate and relevant: C. memnon has the highest ratio of 27.33, correctly representing *with eyespots are significantly more common than wings without eyespots, with ratios as high as* **27.33 to 1**.
    B) Accurate but not the highest: M. peleides has a high ratio of 9.00, but it's not the highest in the data set.
    C) Inaccurate: H. erato has a ratio of 0.11, which indicates wings without eyespots are more common, contradicting the statement.
    D) Inaccurate: This presents raw numbers, not a ratio. The correct ratio for D. plexippus is 0.25, which is low and doesn't support the claim.

    Choice A best completes the text logically and accurately uses the data. It demonstrates the highest ratio of wings with eyespots to those without ($82:3 \approx 27.33:1$), supporting the claim that in some species, wings with eyespots are significantly more common, with ratios as high as stated in the choice.

16. **Answer: C. IDP.** Start with the choice containing a semi-colon. You will notice that the semi-colon separates two sentences: Sentence 1 = *Carved...living* and Sentence 2 = *her eco-conscious...compelling*. Choosing any other option would create a run-on or a comma splice. Choice B needs a comma before the word *and*.

17. **Answer: A. Subject-verb.** The answer choices must connect to its subject noun, which is *vertebrates*. Since it's plural, the subject noun must take the plural verb **comprise**. Also notice that Choice A is the only plural.

    A) comprise - plural
    B) comprises - singular
    C) has comprised - singular
    D) comprised - both

    If you have no idea how to find it, it's usually the odd man out between singular and plural verbs.

18. **Answer: D. Modifier.** The sentence begins with *A pioneer in the field...* This means that the words that immediately follow the comma must be the person who is a pioneer in the field; Choice D correctly cites **Danish physicist Niels Bohr.**

19. **Answer: B. Punctuation.** Start with D. A semi-colon should have an independent clause on both sides. Eliminate D; the construction to the right is not an independent clause. The word **benefit** is functioning as a transitive verb, meaning that it has to take an object. Since it is functioning as a transitive verb, you cannot place a punctuation in between the word and the objects that it benefits. Eliminate A and C for that reason.

20. **Answer: B. IDP.** Start with B. It contains a period, which means there should be a sentence to the right and left of the punctuation. You will notice that there are indeed two sentences: Sentence 1 = *French...research* and Sentence 2 = *Findings...unimaginable.* Since there are two sentences, only choices B and D can work. Eliminate A and C. Now, the colon usually clarifies a term preceding the colon, but Sentence 2 is not intended to clarify, but to add more information. Eliminate D.

21. **Answer: B. Punctuation.** Notice that A, B, and C contain a terminal punctuation—a semi-colon or a period—to separate sentences. Indeed, both sides of the punctuation, regardless of where you insert *unfortunately* contain independent clauses, necessitating a colon or a period. Therefore, we eliminate D since it creates a comma splice. Now, eliminate A and B since the only difference is between the period and a semi-colon (remember, you can eliminate both when you see that option). Choice B properly inserts *unfortunately* in the second sentence to contrast with the first.

22. **Answer: D. Punctuation.** First, notice that the word *such* must connect to the word **as.** No punctuation should separate them. Eliminate B and C. Next, eliminate A because the word **journals** is not a part of the list of standards it must uphold.

23. **Answer: C. Transitions.** Let's analyze the relationship between the two parts of this passage: The first part acknowledges that Charles Darwin wasn't the first to propose evolution. The second part emphasizes Darwin's significant contributions to biology. We need a transition that allows for both these ideas to coexist, showing that while Darwin wasn't first, he was still revolutionary. Let's examine each option:

A) "as a result," - This doesn't work because Darwin's contributions weren't a result of him not being the first to propose evolution. These are separate facts, not cause and effect.

B) "in other words," - This isn't appropriate as the second part isn't restating or clarifying the first part. It's introducing new information about Darwin's contributions.

C) "though," - This is the best choice as it indicates a contrast or concession. It acknowledges that while Darwin wasn't first with the idea of evolution, he still made groundbreaking contributions.

D) "in addition," - This doesn't fit well because the second part isn't simply adding information to the first part. It's presenting a contrasting idea that needs to be balanced against the first statement.

The most logical transition would be "though" (option C) as it best captures the relationship between the two parts of the passage. It allows for the acknowledgment that Darwin wasn't first while still emphasizing his crucial contributions to biology. This transition conforms to the conventions of Standard English by properly connecting these two related but contrasting ideas.

24. **Answer: D. Transitions.** Let's analyze the relationship between the parts of this passage about the Renaissance: The first part introduces the Renaissance as a period of artistic and scientific achievements in Europe, mentioning great thinkers and artists emerging during this time. The second part, which needs a transition, discusses the renewed interest in classical learning and its impact on literature, philosophy, and education. We need a transition that logically connects these ideas, showing how the renewed interest in classical learning relates to the previously mentioned achievements of the Renaissance. Let's examine each option:

A) "Subsequently," - This doesn't work well because the renewed interest in classical learning wasn't necessarily a chronological follow-up to the achievements mentioned. The Renaissance was characterized by concurrent developments in various fields.

B) "In contrast," - This is inappropriate because the renewed interest in classical learning isn't contrasting with the previously mentioned achievements. It's actually complementary to them.

C) "In fact," - This could work as it can be used to introduce additional, supporting information that reinforces or expands on the previous statements about Renaissance achievements.

D) "Furthermore," - This is the best choice as it smoothly adds more information about the Renaissance, logically extending the discussion from artistic and scientific achievements to include the revival of classical learning.

The correct transition word here would be **Furthermore**, as it best connects the ideas in the passage. It indicates that the renewed interest in classical learning is an additional, related aspect of the Renaissance, building upon the artistic and scientific achievements already mentioned.

25. **Answer: B. Rhetorical synthesis.** Find the answer that supports the question stem: **specify the different backgrounds of the two prize-winning authors.** Eliminate Choice A; it focuses on the titles of the winning novels and the authors' names without specifying their different backgrounds. Eliminate Choice C; it mentions that both authors are from immigrant backgrounds but doesn't specify the differences between their backgrounds. Eliminate Choice D; it discusses the novels and the authors' immigrant backgrounds generally, without specifying the differences between the two authors. Choice B properly specifies the different backgrounds of the two prize-winning authors, as

evidenced by the specific phrases: **Junot Díaz, of Dominican descent** and **Viet Thanh Nguyen, of Vietnamese descent**. It also includes the relevant information about their **Pulitzer** wins in **2008** and **2016** respectively, providing additional context that differentiates the authors.

26. **Answer: D. Rhetorical synthesis.** Find the answer that supports the question stem: **compare the replicability of the cognitive biases study and the memory formation study.** Eliminate Choice A; it includes irrelevant information about the decision-making processes study. Eliminate Choice B; it incorrectly states the cognitive biases study is not replicable, rather than poorly replicable. Eliminate Choice C; it compares the wrong studies (decision-making and cognitive biases). Choice D properly compares the replicability of the two specified studies, as evidenced by the specific phrases: **study on memory formation is considered highly replicable** and **study on cognitive biases falls in the poorly replicable range**. These phrases directly correspond to the information in the notes about the RI scores (6 for memory formation, 2 for cognitive biases) and their interpretations on the ten-point scale.

27. **Answer: A. Rhetorical synthesis.** Find the answer that supports the question stem: **make a generalization about the types of coffee beans used in commercial coffee production.** Eliminate Choice B; it compares Arabica and Robusta beans but doesn't generalize about their use in commercial production. Eliminate Choice C; it discusses coffee's popularity and caffeine content without addressing commercial production. Eliminate Choice D; it compares the characteristics of Robusta and Arabica beans but doesn't generalize about their commercial use. Choice A properly makes a generalization about coffee bean types in commercial production, as evidenced by the specific phrases: **different beans are used** and **often blended to balance quality and cost**. This generalization effectively synthesizes the information from the notes about the two main coffee species (Arabica and Robusta), their different characteristics, and their combined use in commercial blends.

TEST 4: MODULE 2 ANSWER EXPLANATIONS

1. **Answer: C. Sentence completion.** The clues are *revolutionized the art world* and *innovative techniques and subjects*. This suggests that the Impressionist movement introduced something new and different, opposing established academic traditions. Therefore, the movement would have rejected these traditions. The word **rejected** means to refuse to accept or support something, which accurately describes the Impressionists' stance towards academic traditions. Eliminate Choice A; **invented** means to create or design something that has not existed before. Eliminate Choice B; **misinterpreted** means to understand or explain something incorrectly. Eliminate Choice D; **recanted** means to withdraw or disavow a previous statement or belief.

2. **Answer: C. Sentence completion.** The clues are *intriguing disparity* and *have attracted notably less scientific attention*. This suggests a contrast between the amount of research on surface-dwelling fish species and deep-sea organisms, with the former having more studies. This implies that studies on surface-dwelling fish species are abundant or numerous. The word **copious** means plentiful in number, which accurately describes the state of research on surface-dwelling fish species. Eliminate Choice A; **sporadic** means occurring at irregular intervals or only in a few places; scattered or isolated. Eliminate Choice B; **tentative** means not certain or fixed; provisional. Eliminate Choice D; **ambivalent** means having mixed feelings or contradictory ideas about something or someone.

3. **Answer: C. Sentence completion.** The clues are *expansion of physics research* and *foundation of modern nuclear physics*. This suggests that the laboratories from the era after 1896 played a significant role in nuclear physics. However, the phrase *but eighteenth-century experimenters like Benjamin Franklin should be considered just as crucial* implies that the importance of post-1896 research might be overstated. The word **an outsized** means disproportionately large, which accurately describes the perceived importance of these laboratories in relation to earlier work. Eliminate Choice A; **a volatile** means liable to change rapidly and unpredictably, especially for the worse. Eliminate Choice B; **a tenacious** means tending to keep a firm hold of something; clinging or adhering closely. Eliminate Choice D; **an infinitesimal** (corrected spelling) means extremely small.

4. **Answer: D. Vocab in context.** The clues are *overgrown hedge* and *thorny tendrils*. The phrase *argued every inch of our advance* is used metaphorically to describe the hedge's resistance to their progress. This suggests that the hedge is actively hindering their movement forward. The word **prevented access to** most accurately captures this meaning in the context. The hedge is physically obstructing their path, not engaging in a debate or verbal argument. Eliminate Choice A; **debated with** implies a verbal exchange, which doesn't fit the context of a physical obstruction. Eliminate Choice B; **complained about** suggests verbal expression of dissatisfaction, which doesn't match the physical nature of the hindrance. Eliminate Choice C; **reasoned against** implies logical argumentation, which is not applicable to a plant's physical obstruction.

5. **Answer: C. Global Structure.** Use process of elimination by evaluating each separate component in the answer choice.

A) It details atmospheric methane increases and temperature changes - ACCURATE, explores ocean-driven weather pattern shifts - ACCURATE, and identifies an unexpected cause for these changes - INACCURATE. The passage does not mention any unexpected causes for the changes. It presents findings but does not discuss causality.

B) It analyzes Arctic methane increases and corresponding temperatures - ACCURATE, explains the consequence of jet streams on ocean warming - INACCURATE, and documents the impact on two species - ACCURATE. The passage states that ocean warming affects jet streams, not the other way around as this choice suggests.

C) It finds a correlation between atmospheric gas and temperature - ACCURATE, explores the impacts of warming in the Arctic Ocean - ACCURATE, and examines wildlife trends and adaptations - ACCURATE.

D) It introduces notable trends in the Arctic Ocean - INACCURATE, analyzes the results of alterations in the marine current - INACCURATE, and compares conservation efforts for two Arctic species - INACCURATE. The passage begins with atmospheric changes, not ocean trends. It discusses jet streams, not marine currents. It mentions wildlife population changes and behaviors but does not compare conservation efforts.

6. **Answer: C. Details.** The question asks about experts' reservations regarding CCS, which links to the excerpt where *environmental scientists caution that the long-term viability of underground CO2 storage remains unproven, and the energy-intensive nature of the capture process may offset a significant portion of the emissions savings*. Use process of elimination. We can eliminate Choice A because the text states that CCS *could reduce CO2 emissions by up to 90%*, contradicting the idea that the technology is **not sufficiently advanced to capture a meaningful amount of CO2 emissions**. Choice B is eliminated as the text doesn't mention **concerns about the safety of transporting captured CO2**. Choice D is incorrect because while the text mentions high capital costs, it doesn't suggest that these costs **can be offset by its long-term economic viability**. Choice C is correct as it accurately reflects the reservations in the text: the *long-term viability of underground CO2 storage remains unproven* addresses the **sustained effectiveness of CO2 storage**, and the *energy-intensive nature of the capture process may offset a significant portion of the emissions savings* relates to the **net environmental benefit are subject to debate**.

7. **Answer: D. Details.** The question asks about the relationship between quantum mechanics and information theory, which links to the excerpt: *Intriguingly, this principle has parallels in information theory, manifesting as a trade-off between message length and transmission accuracy. In communication systems, maximizing data throughput often increases error rates, mirroring quantum mechanical constraints*. Use process of elimination. We can eliminate Choice A because while the text discusses limitations in quantum systems, it doesn't suggest that information theory specifically exhibits **limitations in completeness**. Choice B is incorrect as the passage doesn't indicate that **information theory overcomes constraints** in quantum systems; rather, it suggests they have similar constraints. Choice C is eliminated because the text doesn't state that **information theory and quantum systems were developed as an application** of a fundamental principle; it only notes parallels between them. Choice D is correct as it accurately reflects the passage's main point: *this principle has parallels in information theory* and *mirroring quantum mechanical constraints* suggest that **both quantum systems and information theory exhibit similar constraints on two shared**

and fundamental aspects (precision of measurement in quantum mechanics, and the trade-off between message length and accuracy in information theory).

8. **Answer: D. Details.** The question asks about factors shaping coral reef ecosystems, which links to the excerpt: *Dr. Tanaka's research on the Great Barrier Reef demonstrated that coral health directly influences both predator and prey populations, often overriding traditional predator-prey dynamics. Similarly, Dr. Chen's work in the Caribbean found that seasonal water temperature fluctuations were the primary driver of species distribution patterns, with predation pressure playing a secondary role.* Use process of elimination. We can eliminate Choice A because while the text mentions **seasonal water temperature fluctuations**, it doesn't suggest they shape complex interactions between coral reef systems and predator and prey; rather, it states they drive species distribution patterns. Choice B is incorrect as the passage doesn't directly compare the significance of **coral reef structure** to seasonal water temperature variations; it presents them as separate findings from different studies. Choice C is eliminated because while the text mentions both factors, it doesn't state that **the complex interplay between water temperature fluctuations and predation pressure create species distribution patterns**; instead, it presents temperature as primary and predation as secondary. Choice D is correct as it accurately reflects the passage's main points: *coral health directly influences both predator and prey populations* and *seasonal water temperature fluctuations were the primary driver of species distribution patterns* suggest that **the combined influence of coral health and seasonal temperature variations affect the distributions of predator and prey populations**.

9. **Answer: D. Supporting claims.** The claim to support is that *related diversification generally leads to higher brand loyalty compared to unrelated diversification*. We can eliminate Choice A because it contradicts the claim, showing higher loyalty for unrelated diversification. Choice B is eliminated as the difference in loyalty between related and less related diversification is minimal. Choice C doesn't clearly distinguish between related and unrelated diversification, making it unsuitable. Choice D strongly supports the claim: **"Related diversification generally leads to higher brand loyalty"** = *A meal kit company's introduction of online cooking classes was adopted by 78% of its existing customers*, while **"compared to unrelated diversification"** = *whereas its expansion into a line of casual clothing only attracted 15%*. This example clearly demonstrates a higher adoption rate (implying brand loyalty) for related diversification compared to unrelated diversification, strongly supporting Dr. Chen's conclusion.

10. **Answer: A. Infographics.** Use process of elimination. Eliminate choice B as PBL didn't show consistently higher scores across all skills. Eliminate choice C as PBL didn't demonstrate higher creativity. Choice D, while factually correct about PBL's highest and lowest scores, is irrelevant; it doesn't effectively explain PBL's overall superiority. Choice A provides the most comprehensive and balanced view of the data, acknowledging both PBL's strengths and its weakness, which aligns with the researchers' conclusion of PBL's overall superiority. Choice A most effectively uses the data from the table to support the conclusion that PBL is superior to TL because **it resulted in higher critical thinking and problem-solving scores, despite lower creativity scores**. The data shows that for critical thinking, PBL scored higher (7.8) than TL (6.5), and for problem-solving, PBL matched TL (both 7.1). Although PBL scored lower in creativity (6.9) compared to TL (7.7), this choice accurately

represents PBL's overall performance.

11. **Answer: A. Supporting claims.** The claim to support is that *neutrophils play a more critical role in the early stages of bacterial infections compared to viral infections*. We can eliminate Choice B because it contradicts the claim, showing neutrophils peaking earlier in viral infections. Choice C is eliminated as it doesn't distinguish between bacterial and viral infections. Choice D, while showing a difference, doesn't address the timing aspect of the claim. Choice A strongly supports the claim: **"neutrophils play a more critical role"** = *depletion of neutrophils led to a significant increase in bacterial load*, while **"in the early stages of bacterial infections compared to viral infections"** = *within 6 hours of infection, while viral titers were not significantly affected until 24 hours post-infection*. This example clearly demonstrates a more immediate and critical role of neutrophils in bacterial infections compared to viral infections, strongly supporting Dr. Selim's conclusion.

12. **Answer: C. Supporting claims.** The claim to support is that *the fear of the unknown after death prevents people from ending their lives*. We can eliminate Choice A because while it introduces Hamlet's contemplation, it doesn't address the fear of the unknown after death. Choice B is eliminated as it focuses on death as an escape from life's troubles without emphasizing the fear preventing suicide. Choice D, while related to overthinking preventing action, doesn't specifically address the fear of the unknown after death. Choice C strongly supports the claim: **"fear of the unknown after death"** = *"But that the dread of something after death, / The undiscovered country from whose bourn / No traveler returns"*, while **"prevents people from ending their lives"** = *"puzzles the will"*. This quotation directly expresses the fear of what comes after death and how it hinders the will to act, strongly supporting the claim presented in the question.

13. **Answer: D. Logical completion.** Identify the line of reasoning: 1) The International Language Acquisition Project (ILAP) is a large-scale, long-term study across 30 countries. 2) ILAP requires a large team and generates vast amounts of data. 3) A single-site vocabulary assessment on preschoolers over six months is described as relatively straightforward. 4) The question implies a contrast in logistical challenges between the two types of studies. Eliminate Choice A; it focuses on the diversity of ILAP's sample, which doesn't address the logistical contrast. Eliminate Choice B; it introduces an unsupported claim about the reliability of longitudinal studies versus short-term research. Eliminate Choice C; while potentially true, it doesn't explain the difference in logistical challenges. Choice D logically completes the text because *a single-site vocabulary assessment can be conducted without complex coordination* directly addresses why the focused, short-term research **may not face the same logistical challenges**. This choice highlights the key difference between the complex, multi-site ILAP study and the simpler, single-site assessment, explaining the relative ease of the latter in terms of logistics and coordination.

14. **Answer: B. Weakening claims.** The claim to weaken is that *higher energy can lead to increased boson detection*. We can eliminate Choice A because it results in a net zero change: *amplify the effect of beam luminosity and collision frequency on both the production of Higgs bosons and the rate of background particle generation*, implying equal increases in signal and noise. Choice C is eliminated as it also results in a net increase in detection abilities. Choice D is eliminated as it leads to a net increase in detection abilities: *heighten luminosity and accelerate collision frequency but have no*

effect on the rate of background particle production. Choice B strongly weakens the claim: **"background noise is likely to increase"** = *they raise the rate of background particle production,* while **"if the collider increases its energies"** is directly addressed by *Higher collision energies.* Importantly, *Higher collision energies suppress luminosity and subdue collision frequency* results in a net decrease in the signal-to-noise ratio. This net decrease occurs because while the signal (Higgs boson detection) is reduced due to suppressed luminosity and collision frequency, the background noise increases.

15. **Answer: D. Logical completion.** Identify the line of reasoning: 1) Oxidative stress affects cellular organelles, as shown in Chen and Lee's 2018 study on mitochondria in fibroblasts. 2) A meta-analysis found observable differences in organelle parameters between stressed and unstressed groups across all studies. 3) On average, mitochondria studies showed larger differences than endoplasmic reticulum studies. 4) For every organelle, some individual studies showed differences above the mitochondria average. Now eliminate. Eliminate Choice A; it introduces a comparison between Chen and Lee's specific study and the meta-analysis average, which isn't supported by the given information. Eliminate Choice B; it introduces new information about the reversibility of effects, which isn't mentioned in the passage. Eliminate Choice C; it contradicts the statement that mitochondria studies showed larger differences on average than endoplasmic reticulum studies. Choice D logically completes the text because *some studies of endoplasmic reticulum found larger effects of exposure to oxidative stress than some studies of mitochondria did* directly follows from the statement that **"for every organelle examined, there were individual studies showing differences well above the average for mitochondria"**. This choice aligns with the information provided and logically extends the comparison between mitochondria and endoplasmic reticulum studies, showing that despite the average trend, individual studies varied widely in their findings.

16. **Answer: A. IDP.** First, start with choice C and determine the components to the left and right of it. A complete sentences rests to the left and a full sentence to the right. This means that you can eliminate Choice B. Next, eliminate Choice D because you need a comma before the **and** in order to join two full sentences (independent clauses). Now, eliminate C because a colon should clarify a general term to the left of it. There's no clarification being done here.

17. **Answer: C. Modifier.** Notice that all the answer choices are different. This is a modifier problem. Look at the beginning of the sentence *Using advanced telescopes.* Whatever follows the comma after *telescopes* should be the object that is using them. Choice C correctly starts with **astrophysicist Dr. Sarah Johnson.**

18. **Answer: D. Verb tense.** Since there are NO singular or plural verbs, this is testing verb tense. Now notice the other verbs that indicate tense: *developed, enabled,* and *regarded.* This means that the correct answer should also be in the past tense. Eliminate A. Now, **had been recognized** is something called a past perfect. You use the past perfect to indicate a time before the past tense in the sentence. It wouldn't make sense here, since he was recognized after he *developed.* Eliminate B. Now, choice C is in the past tense, but in its form, the sentence suggests that he was doing the recognizing, not that others recognized his work. Eliminate C. Choice D uses the word **would** which is the past form of will.

19. **Answer: C. IDP.** The word **that** must connect to the word *prioritizes* in order to complete the idea. The problem with A, B, and D is that none contain a comma to close off the parenthetical, thereby creating a fragment. Notice

    A) The Montessori method is an approach to education that seeks…,prioritizes
    B) The Montessori method is an approach to education that has sought…,prioritizes
    D) The Montessori method is an approach to education that is seeking…prioritizes

    Whereas C creates the connection.

    C) The Montessori method is an approach to education that, seeking to…, prioritizes

20. **Answer: C. IDP.** Start by evaluating the answer choice with the period, Choice C. Notice that there is a full sentence to the left and a full sentence to the right. Eliminate Choice A since it creates a comma splice. Next, eliminate Choices B and D; the word **and** needs a comma before it to combine to independent clauses.

21. **Answer: A. Subject-verb.** Notice that choices B, C, and D are plural verbs and choice A, a singular. Now connect the verb to the subject by first crossing out the comma sandwich *which…Daphne*. Next, cross out the prepositional phrase *of marble…statues*. Now, you're left with the subject noun *assortment* which correctly connects to the singular verb **stands.**

22. **Answer: C. Transitions.** Let's analyze the relationship between the two parts of this passage: the first sentence introduces polysynthetic morphology and its impact. The second sentence introduces analytic morphology and a different impact. We need a transition that allows for both these contrasting ideas to coexist. Let's examine each option:

    A) "Consequently," - This option doesn't work because it implies a cause-and-effect relationship that doesn't exist between the parts.
    B) "In fact," - This option isn't appropriate as it's usually used to introduce a surprising or lesser-known fact, which doesn't apply to the given information.
    C) "Conversely," - This is the best choice as it indicates a contrast or concession. It allows the reader to understand the difference between the effects of polysynthetic and analytic morphology on cognition and cultural adaptation.
    D) "That is," - This option doesn't fit well because the second part isn't simply clarifying or restating the first part. It's presenting a contrasting idea that needs to be balanced against the initial statement.

23. **Answer: D. Transitions.** Let's analyze the relationship between the two parts of this passage: the first part describes the old lighthouse's location atop a rocky cliff and its purpose in warning ships of the dangerous shoreline.
    The second part provides additional information about the lighthouse's environment and the generations of keepers who maintained it. We need a transition that allows for both these ideas to

coexist, showing that the lighthouse's surroundings and the dedicated keepers are part of the same context. Let's examine each option:

A) "Hence," - This option doesn't work because it implies a cause-and-effect relationship that doesn't exist between the parts.
B) "Fittingly," - This option isn't appropriate as it suggests a connection or appropriateness that's not relevant to the context.
C) "In fact," - This option isn't ideal because it's usually used to introduce a surprising or lesser-known fact, which doesn't apply to the given information.
D) "There," - This is the best choice as it serves as an adverb to smoothly connect the two sentences and introduce the context of the lighthouse's surroundings. It maintains the narrative flow while providing additional details about the setting and the lighthouse keepers' dedication to their task.

24. **Answer: A. Transitions.** Let's analyze the relationship between the two parts of this passage: the first part highlights the development of the polio vaccine in the 1950s as a significant milestone in combating the disease, emphasizing its severe effects on children. The second part discusses the challenges faced in achieving the vaccine's widespread success, mentioning that it took years of immunization campaigns and public health efforts to control and eliminate polio in many regions. We need a transition that allows for both these ideas to coexist, showing that despite the initial breakthrough, substantial efforts were required to make the vaccine effective on a global scale. Let's examine each option:

A) "That being said," - This is the best choice as it acknowledges the initial breakthrough mentioned in the first part while introducing the contrasting idea that success was not immediate. It helps maintain the context and flow of the narrative.
B) "Accordingly," - This option doesn't work because it implies a cause-and-effect relationship that doesn't accurately represent the connection between the parts.
C) "Indeed," - This option isn't ideal because it's typically used to emphasize or agree with a point, which doesn't fit the contrasting nature of the second part.
D) "As a result," - This option doesn't fit well because the second part isn't a direct result of the first part. The challenges faced in achieving widespread success are not a consequence of developing the vaccine but rather a separate aspect of the overall story.

25. **Answer: B. Transitions.** Let's analyze the relationship between the two parts of this passage: the first part introduces the Amazon rainforest as the "lungs of the Earth" due to its ability to absorb carbon dioxide and produce oxygen. The second part clarifies this idea, explaining how the process of photosynthesis affects global climate patterns beyond just air purification. We need a transition that allows for both these ideas to coexist, showing that the second part clarifies what it means by the lungs of the earth. Let's examine each option:

A) "In reality," - This option doesn't work because it implies that the first statement is misleading or not entirely true, which isn't the case here.

B) "In fact," - This is the best choice as it introduces clarifying information that reinforces and expands upon the initial statement about the Amazon's role. It helps maintain the context and flow of the explanation.

C) "In turn," - This option isn't ideal because it suggests a cause-and-effect relationship or a sequence of events, which doesn't accurately represent the connection between the parts.

D) "In addition," - While this option could work, it's not providing additional facts as it is explaining how it is important.

26. **Answer: C. Rhetorical synthesis.** Find the answer that most effectively emphasizes when and where the Ostwald process was first implemented. Eliminate Choice A; it focuses on Ostwald's general contributions to chemistry **made significant contributions to physical chemistry and catalysis** without mentioning the implementation of the Ostwald process. Eliminate Choice B; while it mentions the patent date **patented in 1902**, it doesn't specify where the process was first implemented. Eliminate Choice D; it provides general information about the Ostwald process and its developer **developed by the renowned German chemist Wilhelm Ostwald** but doesn't address when or where it was first implemented. Choice C correctly emphasizes both when and where the Ostwald process was first implemented, as evidenced by the specific phrases: **In 1902** and **first put into practice at a factory in Gerthe, Germany**. This choice effectively combines information from two of the notes: *The process was first patented on October 17, 1902* and *It was initially implemented at a factory in Gerthe, Germany*. By linking the patent year with the location of first implementation, this answer most effectively meets the goal of emphasizing both the time and place of the Ostwald process's initial use.

27. **Answer: A. Rhetorical synthesis.** Find the answer that most effectively specifies the size and location of the Great Barrier Reef. Eliminate Choice B; while it mentions the size **covers approximately 344,400 square kilometers**, it doesn't provide the location and instead discusses fish species. Eliminate Choice C; it provides the location **Located off the coast of Queensland in northeastern Australia** but mentions the reef's age instead of its size. Eliminate Choice D; it focuses on threats to the reef **threatened by climate change and coral bleaching** without addressing either size or location. Choice A correctly specifies both the size and location of the Great Barrier Reef, as evidenced by the phrases: **covers approximately 344,400 square kilometers** and **off the coast of Queensland in northeastern Australia**. This choice effectively combines information from two of the notes: *The reef covers an area of approximately 344,400 square kilometers* and *It is located off the coast of Queensland in northeastern Australia*. By linking the reef's size with its precise location, this answer most effectively meets the goal of specifying both the size and location of the Great Barrier Reef.

Made in United States
Troutdale, OR
02/16/2025

29015253R00084